Taste of Korea

D1613825

Taste of Korea

over 80 deliciously fiery, aromatic and robust recipes, from classic dishes to regional cooking and sizzling street food, shown in 350 inspiring photographs

Young Jin Song

This edition is published by Aquamarine, an imprint of Anness Publishing Ltd, Hermes House, 88–89 Blackfriars Road, London SE1 8HA; tel. 020 7401 2077; fax 020 7633 9499

www.aquamarinebooks.com; www.annesspublishing.com

If you like the images in this book and would like to investigate using them for publishing, promotions or advertising, please visit our website www.practicalpictures.com for more information.

UK distributor: Book Trade Services; tel. 0116 2759086; fax 0116 2759090; uksales@booktradeservices.com; exportsales@booktradeservices.com
Australian distributor: Pan Macmillan Australia; tel. 1300 135 113; fax 1300 135 103; customer.service@macmillan.com.au
New Zealand distributor: David Bateman Ltd; tel. (09) 415 7664; fax (09) 415 8892

Publisher: Joanna Lorenz
Editorial Director: Judith Simons
Project Editors: Lucy Doncaster and Emma Clegg
Editorial Reader: Rosie Fairhead
Designer: Simon Daley
Illustrator: Robert Highton
Photography: Martin Brigdale
Food Stylist: Lucy McKelvie
Prop Stylist: Helen Trent
Production Controller: Claire Rae

NOTES

Bracketed terms are intended for American readers.

For all recipes, quantities are given in both metric and imperial measures and, where appropriate, in standard cups and spoons. Follow one set of measures, but not a mixture, because they are not interchangeable.

Standard spoon and cup measures are level. 1 tsp = 5ml, 1 tbsp = 15ml, 1 cup = 250ml/8fl oz.

Australian standard tablespoons are 20ml. Australian readers should use 3 tsp in place of 1 tbsp for measuring small quantities.

American pints are 16fl oz/2 cups. American readers should use 20fl oz/2.5 cups in place of 1 pint when measuring liquids.

Electric oven temperatures in this book are for conventional ovens. When using a fan oven, the temperature will probably need to be reduced by about 10–20°C/20–40°F. Since ovens vary, you should check with your manufacturer's instruction book for guidance.

The nutritional analysis given for each recipe is calculated per portion (i.e. serving or item), unless otherwise stated. If the recipe gives a range, such as Serves 4–6, then the nutritional analysis will be for the smaller portion size, i.e. 6 servings. The analysis does not include optional ingredients, such as salt added to taste.

Medium (US large) eggs are used unless otherwise stated.

Front cover shows Seafood and Spring Onion Pancake – for recipe, see pages 30–1.

ETHICAL TRADING POLICY

At Anness Publishing we believe that business should be conducted in an ethical and ecologically sustainable way, with respect for the environment and a proper regard to the replacement of the natural resources we employ.

As a publisher, we use a lot of wood pulp in high-quality paper for printing, and that wood commonly comes from spruce trees. We are therefore currently growing more than 750,000 trees in three Scottish forest plantations: Berrymoss (130 hectares/320 acres), West Touxhill (125 hectares/305 acres) and Deveron Forest (75 hectares/185 acres). The forests we manage contain more than 3.5 times the number of trees employed each year in making paper for the books we manufacture.

Because of this ongoing ecological investment programme, you, as our customer, can have the pleasure and reassurance of knowing that a tree is being cultivated on your behalf to naturally replace the materials used to make the book you are holding. Our forestry programme is run in accordance with the UK Woodland Assurance Scheme (UKWAS) and will be certified by the internationally recognized Forest Stewardship Council (FSC). For further information about this scheme, go to www.annesspublishing.com/trees

Previously published as *Korean Cooking*

PUBLISHER'S NOTE

Although the advice and information in this book are believed to be accurate and true at the time of going to press, neither the authors nor the publisher can accept any legal responsibility or liability for any errors or omissions that may have been made nor for any inaccuracies nor for any loss, harm or injury that comes about from following instructions or advice in this book.

Contents

Korea: an introduction

A country of vibrant contrasts, the experience of Korea embraces the light-filled bustling modern cities, natural landscapes and traditional cultures. Its geography and seasonal changes dictate how to work the land, a mixture of arable, rice and cattle. The diversity of Korea also unfolds within the country's eating traditions, showing the influence of Buddhism and Confucianism, the use of seasonal local ingredients and the culture of sharing multiple dishes.

Korea is a fascinating blend of the fiercely traditional and the breathtakingly modern. The great cities are like neon tigers, with skyscrapers soaring into the air. Seoul's lights shimmer and sparkle, reflected in the waters of the Han River, and everywhere there is a vibrant sense of a thriving, prosperous, 21st-century society. But look closely in the shadows of the towering buildings and there are traces of the Korean heritage. Ancient temples, fortresses and ornate gateways nestle among the high-rise architecture of glass and steel. The furious modern pace is tempered by an aged serenity, and, on leaving the metropolis, you begin to understand why Korea is described as the Land of Morning Calm.

Outside the cities, cloud-enshrouded mountains dominate the landscape, blanketed by lush meadows and dotted with picturesque villages. Working monasteries open their doors to visitors, and the friendly locals welcome travellers enthusiastically.

It is this blend of diverse terrain, venerable history and generosity of spirit that gives the national cuisine its unique identity. Korean cooking is an enticing fusion of flavours and textures, mixing dishes from the simple fare of Buddhist monks with those from the banqueting tables of kings. Centuries of cultural influences combine ingredients and cooking techniques in fascinating ways, making for unfamiliar, delectable meals.

From mild rice dishes and delicate soups, through to zesty pickled vegetables and fiery seafood stews, there is something wonderfully mysterious about Korean food. Whereas the flavours in Chinese and Thai dishes are easily identifiable, Korean cooking blends fresh and preserved ingredients to create complex tastes that constantly surprise and delight.

Every meal comprises multiple dishes, and the entire selection is shared between all the diners. Because of this style of eating there is a real spirit of fellowship when dining Korean style, and this is accentuated by the common practice of cooking food at the table, giving mealtimes an inviting, domestic feel (see also table settings on pages 13–15).

Terrain and climate

The Korean peninsula, in north-east Asia, is bordered by China and Russia to the north and stretches out towards Japan to the south-east. The terrain is both rugged and beautiful, and the climate comprises harsh extremes: monsoon rains in the blazing heat of the summer and deep snow in the freezing winter.

Below *A young farmer near Kyongju, South Korea. Cultivating the land provides many of the key ingredients of Korean cuisine.*

Jagged peaks push up from the sea on all sides, traversed by fresh mountain streams and dotted with lush, grassy plains. Deep valleys give way to sprawling coniferous forests and wide river flats. With this varied environment only around 30 per cent of the land is arable, and half of this is given over to rice cultivation. There is also some cattle grazing.

The peninsula is set in some of the world's best fishing waters, so it is little wonder that seafood is the chief source of protein in the Korean diet. With a sprawling coastline and numerous islands, inlets and reefs, the presence of both a warm and a cold current attracts a great variety of species. The street markets overflow with fish, prawns, crabs, oysters and octopus, and culinary techniques range from drying and pickling through to flame grilling.

Seasonal contrasts

Like other countries in the temperate zone, Korea has four distinct seasons. Spring brings countless hours of sunshine, gentle breezes and azure skies. In summer the weather becomes hot and humid, with heavy monsoon rains from late June. Autumn is dry and cloudless, with plenty of sunlight, followed by the Arctic air of winter, bringing bitter cold, dry weather and snow to the region.

Each of these four seasons provides a variety of ingredients for the Korean kitchen, and certain dishes are traditional at particular times of year. On the hottest days of summer, for example, Koreans eat *samgyetang*, a soup made with chicken, red dates and ginseng, as it is said to provide vitality and stamina to survive the heat. Similarly, *kimchi*, the pickled vegetable dish, is eaten through the long, harsh winters when fresh vegetables are scarce.

Korean cuisine embraces the seasonal variety of its ingredients, and blends the food of the sea, the field and the mountain, reflecting a diverse and bountiful terrain.

Early history

Korea has always been a crossroads of cultures, absorbing the influences of the surrounding countries while developing a distinct national identity. The southern migration of Mongolian tribes to Korea in the 1st century BC brought great change to the country, in both cultural and agricultural terms. The shamanistic beliefs of the Mongols were adopted by the Korean people, as were their cultivation techniques. The Mongols taught the Korean people how to farm the plains and grow crops, and this was to have a tremendous influence on the country's cuisine, resulting in a move away from the seafood that had been a staple of the diet for so long.

Above View of Seoul at night. The neon splendour of the towering modern buildings provides a spectacular contrast to other views that show Korea's rich traditional heritage.

Left A map of North and South Korea. The presence of warm and cold currents around the coastline attracts a variety of fish and shellfish, including mackerel, octopus, squid, prawns, jellyfish, whelks, scallops and crabs. Korea is 30 per cent arable (wheat, maize and rice), half of which is rice cultivation. The mountainous regions include paddy fields, and are also used for herb and spice cultivation. Chillies are another significant part of the Korean harvest.

The introduction of rice

Rice proved itself early in the country's history as a staple ingredient for the Korean diet that was easy to grow in the varying climate. Its inviting taste and the ease with which it could be cooked also had a great effect on the evolution of Korean cuisine. Rice became seen as an essential part of most meals, adopting the same role as bread in the West, and played a major part in establishing the Korean style of eating. It was served as the foundation of the meal, and around this began to grow the idea of using a number of small accompanying dishes of soup, meat, vegetables and seafood.

The influence of Buddhism

From the middle of the 1st century BC Korea began to develop as a country. This was the beginning of the era of the Three Kingdoms: Koguryo, Paekje and Shilla. The kingdoms fought among themselves for dominance until the end of the 7th century AD when Shilla defeated the other two, with Chinese aid, and unified the peninsula under central rule. Korea now entered a long stable period based on Buddhist culture. This had a great effect on the nation's gastronomy, as the slaughtering of animals was prohibited under Buddhist principles.

Diets changed with this dramatic reduction in the consumption of meat, and vegetables took a much more significant role. Temple meals would consist of soup, rice and vegetable dishes, and omitted any strong-smelling ingredients, such as garlic or spring onions (scallions). This influence is still apparent in the *namul* vegetable dishes of modern Korea, and the technique of marinating in soy sauce, rice vinegar and sesame seeds has barely changed. Interestingly, the simple porridge and vegetable dishes of the Buddhist monks have found a new popularity with today's health-conscious citizens.

Confucianism and Chinese influences

This Buddhist culture flourished into the Koryo dynasty (AD935–1392). However, although Buddhism was still prominent, and the monks still wielded influence, the kings of the Koryo dynasty also adopted a Chinese governmental approach, which brought the influence of Confucianism to the country.

Towards the end of the Koryo dynasty the Mongols took control of Korea and ruled for around 100 years before being ousted by the return of General Yi Seong-Gye who established the Chosun (Yi) dynasty in 1392, which ruled until 1910.

Confucianism became the state creed, and the Chinese influence steadily took hold, heralding a new era in the national cuisine. Closer ties with China meant that a wide range of spices and seasonings became available, and this was an important driving influence in determining flavour trends. Black pepper and vinegar were now enjoyed, as were molasses and rice wine.

The Chinese had developed sophisticated techniques for seasoning and cooking meat, mostly derived from the Mongolian use of the barbecue. This was hugely influential on Korean cooking and they adopted the principles while retaining their own traditions. Meat was seasoned and cooked on the barbecue, and then wrapped in vegetable leaves to provide complex flavours and help to create meals that were nutritionally balanced. Documents from this era refer to this style of meal: "In the springtime the wind carries the irresistible scent of wild vegetables over the mountain and the Koryo people enjoy meat with fresh green leaves." This concept of wrapping meat in green leaves influenced the Chinese in turn, and seafood wrapped in lettuce leaves remains a popular dish in China today.

Below Waitresses walking through Namdaemun market in Seoul. This famous market bustles day and night, with meals delivered to the hungry market-stall owners at all hours.

Healthy eating

Since the 17th century the Koreans have been increasingly preoccupied with food and health. Various documents were written on farming and horticulture, and new ingredients have been introduced in an effort to promote a balanced diet.

Sweet potatoes, for example, were brought from Japan in the 18th century to help stave off famine, and quickly became a common ingredient. These potatoes were made into noodles, known as *dangmyun*, which are still found uniquely in Korea.

Modern Korean cuisine is rich in seafood, vegetables and grains, and always provides generous amounts of protein and fibre. Most dishes have a moderate number of calories and are low in fat, making for a healthy and well-balanced diet.

The Koreans recognize medicinal qualities in a variety of their foods and beverages, and seasonings and spices are also effective when treating certain ailments. A daily dose of either sea kelp or carrot juice, for example, is recommended for those suffering from high blood pressure, whereas an increased intake of seaweed or vinegar is considered to help prevent a heart attack. Asthmatics are recommended Asian pears, apricot kernels and extracts from the leaves of gingko trees.

With globalization and the influence of the Western food industry Korean cuisine is evolving at a dramatic rate. However, despite these multicultural influences, the basic diet remains the same as it has for centuries.

Left Dried fish on display at the seafood market near Yeongjongdo pier in South Korea.

The chilli pepper

One of the revolutionary events in Korean culinary history was the introduction of the chilli pepper in the 16th century. In 1592 and 1597 the Japanese invaded Korea, but they were eventually beaten off in 1598 with help from the Chinese. Catholic priests from Portugal accompanied the Japanese troops and brought with them the chilli plants and seeds that the Spanish had introduced from the New World. Prior to this, spiciness had been imparted with the Chinese Szechuan peppercorn, but Korean cooks were wholeheartedly seduced by the flavour and heat of the chilli pepper.

The Koreans adored spicy food, and created *gochujang*, a red chilli paste that became a basic ingredient in every kitchen. Countless dishes were built upon its fiery kick, and traditional techniques for preserving vegetables were brought to life with its strong, pungent flavour. Koreans believe that red is a colour which offers protection from the devil, and this may have had a bearing on the all-pervading use of *gochujang* in their cooking.

Below A traditional Korean house with chillies drying in baskets balanced on a pile of logs.

Korean cuisine

The cuisine of Korea is truly the undiscovered gem of Asian cooking: a treasure trove of exotic scents and flavours. There are key flavours such as garlic, ginger and soy sauce, common preparation techniques such as pickling or grilling, and the importance of sharing food with a selection of small dishes. Then there are the signature dishes, such as *kimchi*, *bulgogi* and *namul*.

Despite the cross-cultural exchanges with China and Japan, and the influence they have had on the evolution of Korean cuisine, it remains quite distinct from either. The cuisines of all the countries share the balance of salty, bitter, hot, sweet and sour – the five flavours – but cooking techniques and ingredients create a marked culinary difference between the three.

One might expect the Koreans to stir-fry in a wok like the Chinese, or eat ingredients raw like the Japanese, as these characteristics would be consistent with the similar geographical surroundings that the countries share. However, the Koreans have developed their own methods of cooking, including preservation techniques that give their cuisine a unique array of flavours.

Characteristic flavours

As in Japan, rice, pickles and fish form the basis of the diet. However, the spices and marinades are distinctive to Korea. Food is predominantly seasoned with the traditional key flavours of garlic, ginger, soy sauce, spring onions (scallions) and sesame oil, plus the careful use of sugar and rice vinegar. Delicious spice pastes tend to form the base of most dishes with either the fermented soybean paste, *doenjang*, or the ubiquitous *gochujang* red chilli paste providing the foundation of many recipes.

Traditionally every family would make their own soy sauce, *doenjang* and *gochujang*, storing them in earthenware jars in the back yard. Preparing these

Below In this traditional Korean kitchen cast-iron cauldrons are built into the clay oven, with wood fires kept burning beneath. These ovens were used to cook the vast quantities of rice and soup needed to feed extended Korean families.

three key seasonings was a significant event in the culinary calendar, as without them cooking for the year became all but impossible.

Food preparation techniques are also different from those found in Chinese and Japanese cuisine. Koreans tend to make a combination of freshly prepared and preserved foods, which have a longer lifespan, rather than preparing one dish for each meal. The strong taste of Korean food originates both from the love of pungent flavours, like the red chilli pepper, and from the preservation techniques that allow those flavours to develop and intensify.

In addition Koreans make use of ingredients in different ways to their neighbours; for example, sesame seeds are always toasted before being added to cooking, to emphasize their nutty flavour. By enhancing certain flavours, and mixing fresh and pickled tastes, Korea has found a culinary identity unlike any other in Asia.

Other local ingredients

The heavily mountainous region encourages the growth of culinary and medicinal herbs and plants. The country is the world's largest producer of ginseng, a sweet, liquorice-flavoured root that has been credited with being everything from an aphrodisiac to a restorative. Ginseng is used to make a renowned Korean tea thought to provide enhanced stamina, and to help high blood pressure. Angelica, a peppery herb with edible leaves and roots, and wormwood, a bitter, aromatic herb, also grow abundantly on the high-altitude slopes, and are used in Korean temple cooking and for the treatment of certain illnesses.

A variety of tastes

A typical Korean meal will have a selection of small dishes, rather than a single main dish for each person, and all the food is served together rather than as a first and a main course. A grilled (broiled) meat or fish dish is traditionally accompanied by rice, soup and salad, along with a selection of pickled vegetables. These pickled vegetables, or *kimchi*, are the national food of Korea, and its most famous culinary export. Although any pickled vegetable can be called *kimchi*, the best-known variety is made with *napa* cabbage and its production is an ancient and revered art. The

vegetables are coated with a mixture that typically includes chilli, ginger, garlic, soy sauce and fish paste, and then sealed and left to ferment until the flavours have blended. Koreans pickle most vegetables in this manner, including radishes, cucumber and aubergine (eggplant), as well as fish, shellfish, fruit and almost any other ingredient that comes to hand. During the fermentation process the vegetables lose much of their natural flavour, adopting the tastes of the seasonings, but their texture is greatly enhanced.

Koreans will eat *kimchi* on literally every day of the year and traditionally prepare a large amount during *kimjang* season, which occurs around the time of the autumn harvest. This is an important social event when *kimchi* ingredients are blended together in copious quantities and buried in earthenware crocks, keeping them cool while they ferment over the long winter months. When the jars are opened the contents are imbued with delicious fiery flavours – a perfect contrast to the chill of the wintry weather.

The other signature dish of Korean cuisine is *bulgogi*. High-quality meat – usually beef – is sliced paper-thin and marinated in a blend of soy sauce, sesame seeds, spring onions (scallions) and

Above Handmade earthenware pots under autumnal gingko trees in Korea. These pots were traditionally used to preserve soy sauce, doenjang soybean paste and gochujang chilli paste in the gardens of Korean homes.

ginger. After the flavours have permeated the meat, the beef slices are cooked in a dome-shaped pan placed over a charcoal brazier. The pan has a channel that catches the delicious juices produced during cooking, and they are eaten with rice and vegetables. As the marinade cooks it forms an appetizing glaze over the meat, which is then eaten either with spicy dipping sauce or wrapped in leaves with slices of fresh garlic and green bell pepper.

Grilling (broiling) is a hugely popular method of cooking in Korea, and echoes back to the barbecue techniques introduced by the Mongols. Other cooking practices are generally similar to elsewhere in the world, with stewing, steaming and shallow-frying being the most popular. The notable exception is that hardly any dishes are baked; this is because the traditional Korean kitchen had a wood-fired stove that did not have an oven.

A variety of soups and stews are also an important part of the Korean diet, dramatically contrasting in taste and potency. Many are very simple, having been developed to use whatever was available in times of scarcity due to winter or poor harvests; today they are often hearty blends of meat and vegetables, or based on the local *dangmyun* noodle made from sweet potatoes.

With the stews, or *chige*, much of the cooking is done in a heavy clay pot called a *tukbaege*. Slow cooking allows the flavours to mingle, and produces fabulous casseroles that combine fish or meat with vegetables, seaweed and tofu, brought to the table still bubbling hot.

The role of rice

Rice tends to be a medium grain "sticky" rice as opposed to long or short grain, or the glutinous varieties found elsewhere in Asia. This rice tends to fare much better in the fluctuating climate of Korea, with its shorter growing season and colder weather, than the strains grown in the tropical countries that lie to the south. It is sometimes mixed with barley or soya beans to enhance the flavour and nutritional properties when used in cooking. Rice and grains are also made into noodles, which play a central role in Korean cooking, and are fermented to create some of the nation's most celebrated beverages.

The harmony of opposites

One of the fundamental principles of Eastern philosophy is that of the two universal opposing forces of yin and yang. This concept has a strong influence on Koreans' thinking, and their approach to cooking, and is reflected in the ingredients selected by chefs when preparing dishes with the intention of achieving harmony in flavour, colour and presentation. Traditional Korean cooking uses green, red, yellow, white and black ingredients in equal amounts to ensure evenness in the diet and to reflect the theory of the five elements from traditional Chinese philosophy: wood, fire, earth, metal and water. The dishes will also have harmonizing yin and yang values: hot and spicy yang foods stimulate the body, whereas cool yin foods calm and nourish the system. Neutral foods are a balance of both. Therefore the perfect meal will have yang dishes to heat up the body and yin dishes to cool the brain.

Drinking

Koreans tend to drink mainly water or *boricha*, a tea brewed from roasted barley, with their meals. Drinking green tea is also very popular, a custom that was introduced with the rise of Buddhism in the 7th century as an indispensable part of temple

Below Two friends share a pot of green tea and plate of traditional rice cakes in a tea house in Korea.

ceremonies. During the Koryo dynasty tea became popular among the upper classes and nobility, too, even finding a place in the royal court, and there are tea shops on the streets of Korea today that stem from this imperial tradition.

Aside from tea there is a wide range of alcoholic beverages including the local wine, *chungju*, a variety of domestically brewed beers, and *makgoli*, a potent milky-white rice drink. However, the most famous drink in Korea is *soju*, a rough grain spirit with a fearsome kick, which was traditionally distilled in Buddhist monasteries. The popularity of *soju* cannot be overestimated, and no Korean meal is really complete without a glass of this potent liquor.

In the past, Korean drinking was steeped in convention and ceremony, particularly to show respect to drinking companions. Over time these traditions have relaxed, although there are some basic rules by which all Koreans still abide. One of these is to allow an older person to sit at the most respected seat at the table, which is the one that is closest to the fireplace or with the best view of the entrance.

Koreans will never pour their own drinks, but it is courteous for their companion to pour for them. Both hands are used to receive a drink, and it is more

important to accept the drink than actually to drink it; declining the first glass is considered terribly impolite, and it is better to accept the glass and simply touch it against the lips than to refuse it entirely. The correct amount to drink is a matter of some debate in Korea, and tastes have become more bacchanalian in recent years. However, the traditional wisdom is summed up by an old saying, which translates as "Don't stop after one glass, three glasses is lacking, five glasses is proper and seven glasses is excessive."

Table settings
The classic table setting is one of the most impressive aspects of Korean cuisine and is quite unique, in both its selection of dishes and its form of presentation. As with other Asian countries a bowl of soup and dish of rice are customary for every person dining. However, what sets the Korean table apart from its Oriental neighbours is the fact that all the dishes are served simultaneously rather than as one course after another. The traditional menu, known as *hanjungsik*, calls for a large number of dishes to be served at the same time, with the sheer volume of food making every meal seem like a banquet. For full ceremonial *gungjungsik* meals so many dishes are served that it seems the table legs will buckle under the weight, but this lavishness is characteristic of Korea.

***Left** A pot of green tea. Since the 7th century green tea has been a popular beverage in Korea, and it is still enjoyed as an important element of a meal.*

***Below** A Korean family serving themselves with chopsticks from an impressive array of dishes.*

*Right A 12-chup table for
a gathering of four, with
individual soup dishes and
12 accompanying side dishes.*

The Korean table setting is based around
a complex, historical design, which is rich with
significance. The classic Korean table is round,
symbolizing the sun and the yang virtue, whereas
its four legs point to the ground signifying the yin
properties of the earth. The arrangement and
presentation of the dishes have their origins with
the nobility of the Chosun dynasty, and settings
differ depending on the nature of the occasion and
the traditions surrounding it. During that era the
social status of a household would dictate the
number of dishes they served at each meal, and
this is reflected in modern table settings.

While the idea of sharing an abundance of small
dishes is the same as the Spanish *tapas* style of
dining, the Korean approach requires all the dishes
to complement each other. To this end the recipes
of certain dishes will be altered depending on the
other dishes being served so that all the elements
work in harmony with each other.

*Below Traditional Korean
table setting for a 3-chup
lunch. The main dish can be
rice or noodles, with three
accompanying dishes
completing the setting.*

A traditional table setting should incorporate a
variety of ingredients and tastes, and also display a
diversity of cooking methods. The table setting is seen
as an important element to enjoying Korean cuisine, and
allows dishes to complement one another in terms of
flavour while maintaining a nutritional balance. Although
a Korean table setting covers the practicalities of setting
out plates, bowls and cutlery, the most significant
aspect is that it dictates which dishes are to be served
together. Table settings are normally defined by what
the main dish is, except in the case of ceremonial meals.

The bansang table

The most common table setting is based around
the serving of a bowl of rice as the main dish, known in
Korean as *bansang* or *bapsang*. Directly translated *ban*
or *bap* means cooked rice and *sang* means table, and
this form holds true for other table settings. If the main
dish served were based on noodles, *myun* in Korean,
then the table setting would be *myunsang*, or "noodle
table". There are also more elaborate table settings that
are defined by an occasion, for instance weddings,
birthdays or anniversaries, but these are lavish and have
much more sophisticated rules.

On a traditional *bansang* table setting the main
rice dish would be accompanied by soup, a plate of
kimchi and a selection of side dishes referred to as
chups. The number of side dishes included on the table
is reflected in the name given to the setting, with three,
five, seven, nine and twelve *chup* settings the most
traditional. Historically this figure was a reflection of
social status, with three and five *chup* meals the staple

among the lower classes, and nine *chup* meals reserved for the upper classes and nobility. Twelve *chup* meals, or *surasang*, were only allowed to be served to the king, with the expanse of dishes spread across three separate tables. These more ostentatious menus often took days to prepare and offered a complex blend of warm and cold dishes, with mild and spicy ingredients and a harmony of textures and colours.

Regardless of whether the table has a three or twelve *chup* setting, the notion of harmony is still important, and culinary contrasts are reflected in the choice of dishes. Hot dishes are served alongside cold ones, with mild and spicy ingredients designed to complement one another while exhibiting a conspicuous difference. Crunchy vegetables are offset by velvety stews and porridges, while meat, seafood and vegetables are balanced in equal measure.

Laying the table

While some of the subtleties of Korean table settings may have been lost, the fundamentals still apply. The laying of the table requires that for each person dining a bowl of rice should be set on the left and a bowl of soup on the right. A second row is formed behind these with the dipping sauces and *kimchi*, while the side dishes are placed to flank this arrangement. Hot or cooked dishes go on the right, while cold dishes or fresh vegetables sit on the left. Communal dishes, such as stews and noodle bowls, are placed in the very centre to allow them to be easily shared between all the diners. Koreans believe that eating food from the same bowl makes for closer relationships. It is not considered impolite to ask the host for an individual bowl or plate, but it is a rarity among a people whose Confucian values place significance on fellowship and mutual respect.

A spoon and pair of chopsticks are placed next to each soup bowl to complete the table setting. Unlike most other Asian countries, a spoon rather than chopsticks is the main table utensil. Rice, soups and stews are eaten with the spoon, whereas chopsticks are used for the drier side dishes, although the two are never used simultaneously. This spoon culture provides a marked difference to both China and Japan, where bowls are designed to be small enough to lift and hold close to the mouth when eating. Korean food is served in larger, heavier bowls and it is considered bad manners to pick up tableware while eating.

The preference for spoons over chopsticks is due to the nature of the dishes that make up Korean cuisine. The substantial *chige* casseroles that are so popular rely on using a spoon, as do the various mixed rice and porridge dishes.

Selection of dishes

Although there is no prescribed order for eating the many dishes served at a traditional meal, many Koreans start with a small taste of soup before eating the other dishes. There will normally be a selection that reflects a range of preparation techniques, as well as ingredients. Seasoned vegetables are popular, as are the thick, nourishing *chige* stews. There may be steamed or boiled dishes, with seared seafood and tofu. Meat is grilled (broiled) and, as for *bulgogi*, is usually cooked by the diner him or herself over a small charcoal brazier at the table. Occasionally raw fish dishes will also be served, rather like Japanese sashimi. The formation of menus will vary depending on the number of dishes, and when families hold celebrations the more exotic and glamorous dishes are likely to be served.

All Korean table settings are designed to include a harmonious assortment of dishes, and to enjoy the experience of Korean dining fully this is the perfect approach. Therefore when preparing any of the recipes in this book it is advisable to prepare a number of dishes – maybe three or four – and serve them together with a dish of rice and bowl of soup. This dining style allows the full experience of Korean cooking to be enjoyed as it was intended, and ensures a truly satisfying meal.

Above *An example of a modern five* chup *table setting. Contemporary dining in Korea still maintains the old traditions of sharing all of the main dishes.*

Festivals & celebrations

As in many other Asian countries, particular seasonal dishes and beverages are enjoyed during festivals throughout the year. The country's agricultural society has always placed great importance on the changing seasons, and this was traditionally reflected in the festivals that celebrated these transitions in nature.

Many of the ancient traditional Korean celebrations no longer form an active part of the country's calendar, but some are still enthusiastically observed by the country's modern population.

New Year

February is the time when people celebrate lunar New Year, and enjoy *sujunggwa*, a spiced punch made with dried persimmons and cinnamon. During this celebration Koreans hold memorials for their departed ancestors, and revere their elders with a formal bow. The traditional meal for this day is a soup called *tteokguk*, where long strips of rice cake (flavoured with the aromatic locally produced herb, wormwood) float in a clear beef broth. It is said that you cannot become another year older without eating a bowl of *tteokguk*. Another New Year's feast-day dish is the sumptuous and fragrant stew, *galbi tang*.

First Full Moon Day

In springtime Koreans celebrate the First Full Moon Day, which is known as *Jeongwol Daeboreum*. On this day they perform a series of rituals to help prevent bad luck throughout the forthcoming 12 months, waking at dawn to drink rice wine and crack walnuts while praying for good health over the coming year. The two favourite dishes for *Jeongwol Daeboreum* are *ogokbap*, a recipe of steamed rice mixed with five other grains, and *mugeun namul*, which is a medley of vegetable dishes such as mushrooms, radish leaves and steamed shoots of young bracken.

The Festival of Sambok

During the height of summer the three hottest days are celebrated during the Festival of Sambok. These three days are called *Chobok*, *Jungbok* and *Malbok*,

Below left Girls dancing under lanterns on Lantern Day at Chogyesa Temple in Seoul, South Korea.

Below right South Koreans holding banners during a march to celebrate the birthday of the Buddha on May 26.

and are held in honour of the beginning, middle and end of the lunar calendar's hottest period. The classic dish that is eaten at Sambok is *samgyetang*, which is a soup containing a whole chicken stuffed with rice, ginseng and red dates. These ingredients are believed to help boost stamina, and also to give the population the energy to withstand the blazing heat of this time of year.

Chuseok

In the autumn Koreans hold a day of thanksgiving called *Chuseok*. On this day they visit the graves of their ancestors to give thanks for a plentiful harvest, and to pray for the well-being of their loved ones. As part of the *Chuseok* celebrations crescent-shaped rice cakes, called *songpyeon*, are eaten with a taro soup called *torantang*. The *songpyeon* are

stuffed with beans, nuts and seeds, and then presented at the ancestral memorial service, along with fresh fruit from the recent harvest.

Donji

The winter solstice of *Donji* in late December is the final festival of the year in Korea. This is the shortest day and a herald of the bitter weather that will follow for many months. On this day *patjuk* is eaten, a red bean porridge that contains balls of rice. For Koreans it is the colour of this dish that is of particular significance, as it is an ancient belief that red drives away evil spirits and wards off bad luck. By eating this porridge on *Donji* a long-held tradition claims that the family will then be kept safe from harm throughout the bleak and frosty winter months.

Above *A "Happy Funeral Ceremony" procession with thronging crowds in Puyo, South Korea.*

Key ingredients

The worldwide interest in cuisines of other cultures has made the most obscure of ingredients surprisingly commonplace. Korean cuisine has also changed in a number of ways, utilizing certain Western ingredients for taste and style as the popularity of fusion cooking has grown. However, the distinctive properties of certain authentic ingredients are irreplaceable.

Seasonings

Used to create a distinctive flavour, seasonings also preserve the qualities of the individual ingredients. Known in Korea as *yangyum,* the traditional technique of seasoning requires a mixture of spices blended to be nutritionally beneficial in almost medicinal precision. For Koreans there are five elements that govern a person's health and these have their direct counterparts in cooking flavours: salty, sweet, sour, spicy and bitter. These flavours are used to create balance in both flavour and well-being.

The basic seasonings used to create these five different flavours include salt, soy sauce, gochujang chilli paste, doenjang soybean paste, vinegar and sugar. Aromatic seasonings include ginger, mustard, pepper, sesame oil, sesame seeds, spring onion, garlic and chrysanthemum leaves. Most Korean dishes are cooked with at least six different ingredients and seasonings, producing a complex and distinctive taste.

Below, from left: Short grain rice; sweet potato noodles; thin buckwheat noodles; and handmade flat noodles. These four ingredients provide the foundation for the majority of Korean dishes.

Rice

Short grain rice Called *ssal* in Korean, this is quite different from the fluffy long grain rice that is widely used in many Asian countries. It is however much closer in shape and texture to Japanese rice. It becomes soft and sticky when cooked.

Glutinous or sweet rice Slightly longer than the common short grain rice, this is only used in rice cakes, cookies and other sweet dishes.

Brown rice Brown rice is normally cooked as a mixture with white rice and other grains, and is considered to have better nutritional value than the common short grain variety.

Noodles

Glass noodles Known as *dangmyun,* these delicate strands, similar to bean thread vermicelli, are also known as cellophane noodles. They are often used as the base for noodle soups or stir-fried dishes. Prior to cooking glass noodles must be soaked in cold water to soften. Korean glass noodles are distinctively made from sweet potato and are often added to casseroles to provide volume and richness of flavour and texture.

Buckwheat noodles Thin and brown in colour, this type of noodle is known as *memil.* They have a crunchy texture and are similar in appearance to a softer variety called *momil,* made from wheat flour, better known as the Japanese soba noodle.

Handmade flat noodles Also called *kalguksu*, handmade flat noodles are made from plain flour and are popular in modern cuisine for dishes where a more tender texture is suitable.

Somyun A regular plain flour noodle known as somen in Japanese cooking, these are much thinner than the udon noodle. Often used for noodles served in broth, somyun is the name given to any noodle soup recipe.

Vegetables

Chinese cabbage Called *baechu* or *tong baechu* in Korea, the Chinese cabbage is also commonly known as Napa cabbage. Found in most supermarkets it has a long white leaf, and is unlike other round cabbage varieties. It is the key ingredient for traditional *kimchi*.

Chinese white radish This has the crisp, peppery taste of other members of the radish family. However it can grow to over 30cm (1ft) long, and is thick, similar to a large parsnip. Also known by its Japanese name of *daikon* or its Hindi name of *mooli*, it is simply known in Korea as *moo*. With an inherent spiciness and sweetness it produces a pungent flavour.

Leeks The Koreans use *daepa*, a large indigenous variety of the spring onion (scallion) that is sweeter and more flavourful than the green onion. However *daepa* have the same taste as leeks and the two are interchangeable in Korean cooking.

Spring onions (scallions) The most popular garnish for soups and other dishes in Korean cooking, the spring onion has widespread uses. The Korean variant is virtually identical to the Western equivalent.

Perilla Commonly known as wild sesame leaf, perilla can also be called *kenip*. These wonderfully fragrant leaves are used in many ways, and while they are similar to Japanese *shiso* the flavour is slightly different. The refreshing properties of this herb bring out a naturally fresh taste in many dishes, and it is also used as a wrap for food parcels.

Korean chives These are similar to Chinese chives in terms of flavour and texture and in Korea are called *buchu*. Asian chives are flat green vegetables and are significantly larger than the herb variety more familiar in Western cooking. This delicate vegetable bruises very easily so it should be handled and washed with great care.

Minari This is a small salad leaf with a wonderful aroma, similar in appearance to watercress, and with a long, crunchy stem. It is used in stews and salads, or simply blanched and served with a sweet and sour chilli paste dressing. Minari can normally only be found at Korean stores, but watercress can be substituted.

Chrysanthemum leaves Known as *sukgot* in Korea and cooked following a similar method to spinach, these are aromatic and often used to suppress the smell of fish or other strong odours in certain dishes. With its wonderfully exotic fragrance this herb can only be found in Korean stores, but Italian parsley makes a good substitute.

Mung beans These small, round, green beans are used in mung bean soufflé. The sprouts of the mung bean are also a valuable ingredient, and are used to make a distinctive soup. Korean cooking favours mung bean sprouts over other beansprouts as they have an intense nutty flavour and a pleasing crunchy texture.

Fern fronds Sometimes known as "fiddlehead", these are rarely used in the Western kitchen. Wild ferns can be poisonous, so only use the dried fern fronds available at any Asian store. Used as a key ingredient in *yukgejang* soup, this distinctive plant is also often seasoned and sautéed for salad dishes in Korea.

Above, from left: Chinese cabbage; Chinese white radish; chrysanthemum leaves; and Korean chives. These represent four key ingredients in Korean cooking.

Mushrooms

Shiitake mushrooms These mushrooms, called *pyogo* in Korean, have a flat round cap, and are dark brown with an earthy flavour. Available both fresh and dried, they are cultivated widely in Asia. If bought dried they should be soaked in warm water to reconstitute before use.

Enoki mushrooms Also known as *enokitake* in Japanese, enoki mushrooms have a long, thin stem and tiny cap and an extremely delicate, slightly furry texture. Generally used for garnishing, the stem should be trimmed before use.

Oyster mushrooms Pale grey and fan-shaped, oyster mushrooms are often used for casseroles and stir-fried dishes, being mild in taste and silky in texture.

Spices and flavourings

Garlic This essential aromatic is used for everything from seasoning soup to creating marinades for meat and fish. It is also popular used whole as an accompaniment for grilled dishes.

Ginger The distinctive sweet piquant taste of ginger has made it popular all over Asia. Korean cuisine prefers to combine its taste with that of other ingredients, producing a more subtle flavour.

Ginseng A root best known for its medicinal properties and widely used to make tea, ginseng is also popular for its inclusion in the summer chicken soup *samgyetang*.

Chilli The chilli pepper ranges widely in variety from mild to fiery hot. The pungency of chilli, when combined with garlic, is used to make the national dish of *kimchi*.

Dried chilli A sun-dried red chilli can be used to create a sharp, spicy taste. The dried chilli is also used flaked and whole for garnishing and presentation.

Korean chilli powder This ground sun-dried red chilli is a must-have spice for Korean cooking. The Korean variant is very different from any other type of chilli powder in terms of taste and piquancy, and milder than its Indian counterpart. It is normally only found in Korean food stores and larger Asian supermarkets.

Gochujang This fiercely hot fermented chilli paste is made by adding powdered red chilli and glutinous rice powder to soybean paste and aging this mixture in the sun. With a unique mix of hot, sweet, salty and sour tastes *gochujang* is the most popular and indispensable ingredient in Korean cooking. Traditionally made at home, *gochujang* is now found in every food store in Korea.

Doenjang This fermented soybean paste is more commonly known by the name of miso, although the Japanese equivalent has a slightly milder flavour and paler colour. In Korean cooking *doenjang* is used as a base for soups and many other recipes, to create dipping sauces, and as a seasoning.

Soy sauce A by-product of *doenjang*, soy sauce is the Korean soybean paste and has long been one of the most important foods in Korea. It has been used in Asian cooking since the technique of fermenting soybeans was discovered, and is a staple flavour in much of Eastern cuisine. There are a number of different types, with the fresh variety known as light soy and the aged variety known as dark soy sauce. Light soy is used in soups and to season vegetables, while dark soy sauce is used for roasted, steamed and generally more hearty dishes.

Dried fish These are often used to make the stock that forms the basis of soups and stews in Korean cooking. Dried anchovies, called *myulchi*, are commonly used to flavour dishes and this tiny dried fish is surprisingly versatile. While most commonly used to flavour dishes it is also stir-fried and simmered with soy sauce, then served as a side dish.

Dried shrimps Known in Korea as barley shrimps, dried shrimps, when stir-fried, have a nice crunchy texture and match well with the taste of green chilli.

Fish sauce An essential ingredient for making the classic dish *kimchi* where vegetables are fermented (see page 134) is fish sauce. Any anchovy or fish sauce, available in Asian stores and most supermarkets, can be used, and it has a multitude of uses in Oriental cooking.

Fermented fish Known as *jeotgal* or *joet*, fermented fish are a combination of salted fish and shellfish. This seafood mixture is fermented for two to three months before spices are added to enhance the taste. Often used to add flavour to soups and stews, it is also an alternative to salt when making *kimchi* to provide a more potent taste and aroma.

Mirin Japanese rice wine, or *mirin*, is syrupy and sweet when used in cooking. Traditionally it is used as a marinade in order to make meat more tender and reduce its aroma. *Mirin* can be replaced by *sake* or any other rice wine, although each variety does have a slightly different taste.

Sesame oil An ingredient vital to Korean cuisine, sesame oil has a rich nuttiness that gives way to a dramatic flavour.

Bean oil Widely used in Korean stir-fry dishes, bean oil is colourless and odourless and allows the flavours of the ingredients in a dish to remain distinct. Vegetable or sunflower oil both make acceptable substitutes.

Vinegar This ingredient is an important part of Korean cooking, with apple and cider vinegar being most widely used. Persimmon vinegar is a delicious variant, but can be difficult to find outside Korea.

Sesame seeds Used as both flavouring and a garnish in a vast range of Korean recipes.

Gingko nuts Used in both sweet and savoury dishes, gingko nuts are sometimes served as an alternative to lotus seeds. Grilled and salted, these are a popular snack in Japan and Korea, and once cooked they turn a delicate shade of green.

Red dates Known as *jujube* in Oriental cooking, this medicinal fruit is oblong in shape and turns a reddish brown when ripe. With its sweet flavour and vibrant colour it is often used to garnish dishes, and is a common ingredient in cakes and cookies.

Seaweed Used in Korean cooking for centuries, seaweed has a high vitamin and protein content. There are three kinds of seaweed used: kelp, nori and miyuk. Dried kelp, known as *dashikonbu* in Japanese or *dahima* in Korean, can be found in any Asian store, and has a rich sea flavour which is perfectly suited to making soup stock and salads. Kelp should always be soaked in water before being used in cooking. *Nori* is a dried layer of seaweed, and is the Japanese term for the popular edible seaweed known as *kim* in Korea. It has a colour somewhere between dark blue and black, and is sold dried in small, very thin sheets. It has a crisp texture and salty flavour with a distinctly toasty aroma and is used to make the rice rolls known as *maki* in Japan. *Miyuk* is an edible seaweed, known as *wakame* in Japan. It is much softer than kelp, and has a range of vitamins that promote good circulation. A popular Korean soup, traditionally served at birthday celebrations, is made from *miyuk*.

Below, from left:
Gochujang *chilli paste;* doenjang *soybean paste; fish sauce; and gingko nuts. These essential condiments contribute to the characteristic taste of Korean cooking.*

Rice

The foundation of all Korean meals, from breakfast to dinner, is rice. In combination with soup and vegetables it forms an essential part of a nutritious and satisfying Korean meal. Recipes for two of the most widely eaten rice dishes are given here. These are both examples of staple dishes, and most households keep a steamer on so rice is readily available at any time of the day or night.

As with soup and vegetable dishes, the flavours in Korean rice dishes are understated, and are designed to balance and complement the tastes of the accompanying dishes. Knowing the art of preparing the basic rice recipes that are shown here is an essential requirement for creating the heart of any Korean meal.

A staple dish in the national cuisine for centuries, rice, or *bap* as it is known, is so essential in every meal that it has become synonymous with the meal itself. "Did you have *bap*?" is the common way to ask if an acquaintance has already dined, regardless of the meal they had. Koreans believe that their strength comes from the continuing consumption of rice, and that it greatly enhances their stamina.

Rice is traditionally cooked on its own in the Korean kitchen, although sometimes other grains such as millet and barley are included to enhance the flavour. Beans and chestnuts are occasionally included too, and vegetables are often mixed into the dish before serving. Although rice is a staple food across the whole of Asia, each country has its preferred crop varieties and adds particular seasonings to give dishes a unique identity. Long grain rice is common in China and in Thailand, where jasmine is added to give the characteristic aroma. However, the Koreans, like the Japanese, eat only the sticky short and medium grain varieties and much prefer the simple flavour of plain steamed rice.

Below, from left White short grain rice; mixed grains with dried black beans. Rice dishes form the basis of the Korean cuisine, in the same way as in Japan and China.

Steamed rice

Koreans will conventionally cook rice in a steamer, which can be bought at any Asian food store. However, the same flavour and texture can be created with pan-cooked rice. Short grain Asian rice is the best, although pudding rice can be used as an alternative. Good quality rice will have a visible sheen, and the grains will be free from scratches. **Serves 4**

400g/14oz/2 cups short grain   a drop of sunflower oil
   white rice or pudding rice

1 Rinse and drain the rice in cold water four or five times.

2 Place the rice in a heavy pan and add water (preferably filtered) to about 5mm/$\frac{1}{4}$in above the level of the rice.

3 Add one drop of sunflower oil to give the rice a lustrous shine, and then cover with a lid and bring to the boil.

4 Lower the heat and leave to steam. Do not remove the lid during cooking.

5 After 12–15 minutes turn off the heat and leave the rice, still covered, to steam for a further 5 minutes.

Storing rice Any leftover rice can be stored in the refrigerator, wrapped with clear film (plastic wrap) in order to help preserve the moisture. Don't keep rice for more than a couple of days.

Five-grain rice

Plain steamed rice often has grains, beans and lentils added to create the Korean favourite *ogokbap*. These extra ingredients give more of a crunch to the dish's texture, and impart exotic combinations of flavours. Families will eat *ogokbap* at the first full moon of the year, as it is believed that sharing the dish will bring good luck for the coming year. **Serves 4**

40g/1$\frac{1}{2}$oz/generous $\frac{1}{4}$ cup   50g/2oz/$\frac{1}{4}$ cup sorghum or
   dried black beans or sweet   lentils
   beans   200g/7oz/1 cup short grain
50g/2oz/$\frac{1}{4}$ cup barley   white rice
50g/2oz/$\frac{1}{4}$ cup millet   salt
50g/2oz/$\frac{1}{4}$ cup brown rice

1 Soak the beans, barley, millet, brown rice and sorghum or lentils in cold water for 24 hours. Add the white rice to the soaked grains and beans. Drain and rinse well in cold water.

2 Place the rice in a heavy pan and add water (preferably filtered) to about 5mm/$\frac{1}{4}$in above the level of the rice.

3 Add a pinch of salt, then cover with a lid and bring to the boil.

4 Lower the heat and leave to steam. Do not remove the lid during cooking. After 12–15 minutes turn off the heat and leave the grains, still covered, to steam for a further 5 minutes.

Variations Other ingredients can be added in place of the grains or beans. Soya beansprouts and chestnuts are popular.

Snacks from the bustling city streets

A dazzling range of snacks is available on every street corner in the bustling cities of Korea. Deep-fried golden fritters, succulent steamed dumplings and fishcake skewers are all eaten as quick snacks by busy passers-by, and for every culinary predilection there will be a street vendor to satisfy it.

Known as *pojangmacha,* these street vendors occupy small stands which sell a range of dishes, generally designed to be eaten standing up or on the go. Some stalls are permanent fixtures and have seating areas for the patrons, while others are mobile eateries that can easily be carried – or wheeled – to follow the crowds, while at night the streets are transformed with small tents that materialize to serve the hungry masses. These peddlers often have individually designed equipment to cook the particular delicacies they peddle, with different stands specializing in different types of dish. Spectacular contraptions take to the streets in the winter months as rickety carts transport homemade wood stoves around the busy metropolitan areas.

A popular dish for snacking is roasted sweet potatoes with almond syrup, and these are suspended over the stove in a large revolving drum as they roast, emerging hot, sweet and delicious on a chilly day. Other seasons also have unique specialities: *bingsu*, a dish of syrup-drenched ice flakes piled with sweet red beans, is a refreshing treat in the summer, while warming soups and stuffed pancakes are enjoyed in the autumn.

As with every other aspect of Korean cooking, rice is crucial when creating street snacks, and *tuckboki* stir-fried rice cakes are surely the staple of *pojangmacha* cuisine. These sliced rice cakes are traditionally simmered with vegetables and a piquant sauce; however individual traders may throw in other ingredients of their choosing, including dumplings, fishcakes and hard-boiled eggs. Rice rolls wrapped in seaweed are also popular as a quick bite, and despite the similarity to Japanese *maki* have a quintessentially Korean nutty flavour. The fluffy rice is perfectly offset by the crunchiness of the vegetables, and there is a wonderful kick of chilli and garlic.

Dumplings are another ubiquitous street dish, and make the perfect "finger food" to fill up on before a night out, or as a quick snack on the journey home. Although Korean *mandu* dumplings have their origin in Chinese cooking, they are lighter and more aromatic than their Chinese counterparts, and the variety of different stuffings ensure that meat, seafood and vegetable steamed parcels are always to be had on any busy thoroughfare.

Korean street food has adopted a fusion style over recent years, weaving ingredients and recipes from around the globe with classic Korean tastes to create flavourful and exciting snacks to eat on the go.

This simple yet interesting street dish, called *matang*, is thought to have its origins in Chinese cooking. Deep-fried sweet potato is coated in a sugar syrup with crunchy almonds and sprinkled with black sesame seeds, creating a dish that is both savoury and sweet. **Serves 2**

Sweet potato with almond syrup

3 sweet potatoes, peeled
115g/4oz/½ cup light
   muscovado (brown) sugar
2 almonds, crushed

vegetable oil, for deep-frying
black sesame seeds, to
   garnish

1 Preheat the oven to 200°C/400°F/Gas 6. Cut the sweet potatoes into bitesize slices, then soak them in a bowl of cold water for 15 minutes to help remove the starch. Drain, and place the potato slices on a baking sheet. Cook in the oven for 20 minutes, or until they have softened slightly. The potato should not be cooked through, but have a parboiled texture.

2 Put the sugar in a pan with 120ml/4fl oz/½ cup water. Simmer over medium heat until it has formed a sticky syrup, then remove the pan from the heat and add the crushed almonds. Fill a wok or medium heavy pan one-third full of vegetable oil, and heat over high heat to 170°C/340°F, or when a small piece of bread dropped into the oil browns in 15 seconds. Add the sweet potato. Deep-fry until golden brown, then remove from the pan and drain any excess oil on kitchen paper.

3 Combine the potatoes with the syrup, coating each piece evenly. Transfer to a shallow serving dish and garnish with black sesame seeds before serving.

Per portion Energy 667kcal/2819kJ; Protein 5g; Carbohydrate 124.4g, of which sugars 77.4g; Fat 20.2g, of which saturates 2.5g; Cholesterol 0mg; Calcium 115mg; Fibre 7.6g; Sodium 124mg.

Fishcakes are widely eaten as street snacks as they are hearty, flavoursome and easy to cook. This Japanese-style dish is a classic example, with the tender fishcake cooked on skewers in a rich, seaweed-flavoured soup. Perfect for a quick bite! **Serves 4**

Fishcake skewers in seaweed soup

16 fishcake slices
 or fish balls
16 wooden skewers

For the soup
400g/14oz Chinese
 white radish, peeled
3 sheets dried seaweed
10ml/2 tsp Thai fish sauce

10ml/2 tsp light soy sauce
salt and ground black
 pepper

For the soy dip
60ml/4 tbsp dark soy sauce
5ml/1 tsp sesame seeds
5ml/1 tsp wasabi
 paste, or to taste

1 Pierce each slice of fishcake or fish ball with a wooden skewer, and then set aside.

2 To make the dip, mix the dark soy sauce and sesame seeds in a small dish, adding the wasabi paste to taste.

3 To make the soup, put the radish in a pan with the seaweed and 2 litres/3$\frac{1}{2}$ pints/8 cups water. Bring to the boil and add the Thai fish sauce and soy sauce. Lay the skewered fishcakes in the liquid and boil for 20 minutes, or until the soup has thickened. Season with salt and pepper.

4 Pour a little soup into each bowl and add four fishcake skewers. Serve with the spicy soy dip.

Fishcakes You will find fishcake slices and fish balls are available at most Asian food stores.

Per portion Energy 104kcal/435kJ; Protein 6.4g; Carbohydrate 13.1g, of which sugars 3.1g; Fat 3.2g, of which saturates 0.5g; Cholesterol 13mg; Calcium 105mg; Fibre 1g; Sodium 1468mg.

Seafood & spring onion pancake

90g/3½oz squid
2 oysters
5 clams
5 small prawns (shrimp), shelled
3 scallops, removed from
   the shell
15ml/1 tbsp vegetable oil
5 spring onions (scallions),
   sliced into thin strips
½ red chilli, seeded and cut into
   thin strips
½ green chilli, seeded and cut
   into thin strips
50g/2oz enoki mushrooms, caps
   removed
1 garlic clove, thinly sliced
salt and ground black pepper

For the batter
115g/4oz/1 cup plain
   (all-purpose) flour
40g/1½oz/⅓ cup cornflour
   (cornstarch)
2 eggs, beaten
5ml/1 tsp salt
5ml/1 tsp sugar

For the dipping sauce
90ml/6 tbsp light soy sauce
22.5ml/4½ tsp rice vinegar
1 spring onion (scallion), finely
   shredded
1 red chilli, finely shredded
1 garlic clove, crushed
5ml/1 tsp sesame oil
5ml/1 tsp sesame seeds

Per portion Energy 255kcal/1077kJ; Protein
16.5g; Carbohydrate 33.7g, of which sugars
1.9g; Fat 7.1g, of which saturates 1.4g;
Cholesterol 232mg; Calcium 80mg; Fibre
1.4g; Sodium 613mg.

This pancake makes a great appetizer, with the silky texture of squid and scallops accompanied by the delicate crunch and piquancy of spring onions. The vegetables and seafood stud the surface of the pancake, which is sautéed to a golden crisp while leaving the centre light and moist. **Serves 4**

1 To make the batter, sift the flour into a large bowl. Add the remaining batter ingredients with 200ml/7fl oz/scant 1 cup iced water and whisk lightly until smooth.

2 Wash the squid carefully, rinsing off any ink that remains on the body. Holding the body firmly, pull away the head and tentacles. If the ink sac is still intact, remove it and discard. Pull out all the innards including the long transparent "pen". Peel off and discard the thin purple skin on the body, but keep the two small side fins. Slice the head across just under the eyes, severing the tentacles. Discard the rest of the head. Squeeze the tentacles at the head end to push out the round beak in the centre and discard. Rinse the pouch and tentacles well. (Your fishmonger will prepare squid for you, if you prefer.) Chop the squid into small pieces and place in a bowl.

3 Hold an oyster with the rounded shell up. Push the tip of an oyster knife or short-bladed knife into the hinge of the oyster and twist to prise the shell open. Cut the two muscles inside.

Run the blade between the shells to open them. Discard the rounded shell. Cut the oyster away from the flat shell. Add to the bowl. Repeat with the remaining oyster.

4 Open the clam shells and tip each clam into the bowl. Add the prawns and scallops to the bowl. Season with salt and pepper, and leave to stand for 10 minutes.

5 To make the dipping sauce, combine all the ingredients in a small bowl.

6 Coat a large frying pan with vegetable oil and place over medium heat. Pour one-third of the batter into the pan, ensuring that it is a roughly consistent thickness across the base. Place the spring onions, chillies, mushrooms and garlic on to the pancake and then add the seafood, distributing the ingredients evenly. Pour over the remaining batter and tilt the pan to form an even layer. Sauté, turning when necessary, until the pancake is golden brown on both sides.

7 Slice the pancake into bitesize pieces and serve on a serving plate with the dipping sauce.

Rice seaweed roll with spicy squid

400g/14oz/4 cups cooked rice
rice vinegar, for drizzling
sesame oil, for drizzling
150g/5oz squid
90g/3½oz Chinese white radish,
   peeled and diced
3 large sheets dried seaweed
   or nori

For the squid seasoning
22.5ml/4½ tsp Korean chilli
   powder
7.5ml/1½ tsp sugar
1 garlic clove, crushed
5ml/1 tsp sesame oil
2.5ml/½ tsp sesame seeds

For the radish seasoning
15ml/1 tbsp sugar
30ml/2 tbsp rice vinegar
22.5ml/4½ tsp Korean
   chilli powder
15ml/1 tbsp Thai fish sauce
1 garlic clove, crushed
1 spring onion (scallion), finely
   chopped

Per portion Energy 195kcal/830kJ; Protein
8.8g; Carbohydrate 36.2g, of which sugars
4.8g; Fat 2.8g, of which saturates 0.6g;
Cholesterol 84mg; Calcium 32mg; Fibre 0.4g;
Sodium 312mg.

This Korean favourite, *chugmu kimbap*, is influenced by Japanese *maki*, although the seaweed rolls are served separately from the other ingredients. Cooked rice is wrapped in seaweed, and then served with spicy squid and radish. The fluffy texture and mild taste of the rice roll are nicely set off by the crunch of the radish and distinctive kick of the chilli and garlic seasoning. This delicious snack is perfect when accompanied by a bowl of clear soup. **Serves 2**

1 Put the cooked rice in a bowl and drizzle over some rice vinegar and sesame oil. Mix well, then set aside.

2 Wash the squid carefully, rinsing off any ink that remains. Holding the body firmly, pull away the head and tentacles. If the ink sac is still intact, remove it and discard. Pull out all the innards including the long transparent "pen". Peel off and discard the thin purple skin on the body, but keep the two small side fins. Slice the head across just under the eyes, severing the tentacles. Discard the rest of the head.

3 Squeeze the tentacles at the head end to push out the round beak in the centre and discard. Rinse the pouch and tentacles well. (Your fishmonger will prepare squid for you, if you prefer.) Use a sharp knife to score the squid with a crisscross pattern, and slice into generous pieces about 5cm/2in long and 1cm/½in wide.

4 Bring a pan of water to the boil over high heat. Blanch the squid for 3 minutes, stirring constantly, then drain under cold running water.

5 Combine all the squid seasoning ingredients in a bowl, and then coat the squid. Set aside to absorb the flavours.

6 Put the radish in a bowl, then drizzle over some rice vinegar. Leave for 15 minutes and then drain the radish and transfer to a bowl. Add the radish seasoning ingredients, mix well and chill in the refrigerator.

7 Place a third of the rice on to one of the sheets of seaweed, roll into a long cylinder and wrap it tightly. Then slice the cylinder into bitesize pieces. Repeat with the remaining seaweed sheets.

8 Arrange the rolls on a serving plate and serve with the seasoned squid and radish.

Pan-fried kimchi fritters

A classic appetizer and popular snack, these fritters have a crisp golden coating that encloses a succulent blend of *kimchi* and tofu. The contrast of the crunchy exterior and smooth filling makes a delicious juxtaposition of textures, and the dish is served with a zesty soy dip to help bring out the flavours. **Serves 2**

1 Gently squeeze the *kimchi* to remove any excess liquid. Boil the potato and mash it, adding a little milk if required.

2 Squeeze the water from the tofu, and crumble it into a large bowl. Add the *kimchi*, potato, flour, egg, garlic and seasoning. Mix together thoroughly using your hand, and form into small round patties.

3 Coat a frying pan with the oil and place over medium heat. Add the patties and fry until golden brown on both sides. Remove from the pan and place on kitchen paper to remove any excess oil.

4 To make the dip, mix the soy sauce, sesame oil and lemon juice together, and then serve with the fritters.

Perfect partners An ideal accompaniment is a side dish of diced radish *kimchi* (see page 145); its fresh flavours provide a delicious counterpoint to the fried texture of the fritters.

90g/3½oz cabbage *kimchi*, (see page 143) finely chopped
1 potato
a little milk (optional)
50g/2oz firm tofu
25g/1oz/¼ cup plain (all-purpose) flour
1 egg, beaten
5ml/1 tsp crushed garlic
15ml/1 tbsp vegetable oil
salt and ground black pepper

For the dip
45ml/3 tbsp light soy sauce
2.5ml/½ tsp sesame oil
5ml/1 tsp lemon juice

Per portion Energy 206kcal/863kJ; Protein 8.4g; Carbohydrate 20.9g, of which sugars 3.8g; Fat 10.5g, of which saturates 1.8g; Cholesterol 105mg; Calcium 188mg; Fibre 1.9g; Sodium 583mg.

Seafood fritters with pear & soy dip

Succulent prawns, cod fillet and seasoned crab are all battered and lightly sautéed to create these appetizing golden seafood fritters. The prawn fritters have a mushroom and chilli stuffing, and all the crispy bitesize fritters are served with a delicious pear and soy sauce dip. **Serves 4**

2 eggs, beaten
vegetable oil, for frying
salt and ground black pepper

For the prawn fritters
5 medium-size prawns (shrimp)
juice of ½ lemon
30ml/2 tbsp white wine
2.5ml/½ tsp sesame oil
1 dried shiitake mushroom,
 soaked in warm water for about
 30 minutes until softened
1 green chilli, finely chopped
45ml/3 tbsp plain (all-purpose)
 flour for dusting

For the crab fritters
75g/3oz crab meat
3 oyster mushrooms, finely sliced
¼ green (bell) pepper, finely
 chopped
25g/1oz Korean chives, finely
 sliced
1 garlic clove, thinly sliced
2 eggs, beaten
45ml/3 tbsp plain (all-purpose)
 flour
Extra flour for dusting

For the cod fritters
300g/11oz cod fillet
7.5ml/1½ tsp dark soy sauce
5ml/1 tsp white wine
2.5ml/½ tsp sesame oil
45ml/3 tbsp plain (all-purpose)
 flour for dusting

For the dipping sauce
45ml/3 tbsp light soy sauce
45ml/3 tbsp sugar
1 garlic clove, crushed
10ml/2 tsp pear juice
2.5ml/½ tsp lemon juice

1 Combine all the ingredients for the dipping sauce in a small serving bowl.

2 To make the prawn fritters, hold each prawn between two fingers and gently pull off the tail shell. Twist off the head. Peel away the soft body shell and the small claws beneath. Rinse well and season with salt, pepper, lemon juice, white wine and a dash of sesame oil.

3 When the soaked shiitake mushroom has reconstituted and become soft, drain and finely chop it, discarding the stem. Mix with the chilli, season with a dash of sesame oil and salt, and dust with a little flour. Set the mushroom stuffing aside. Dust each prawn with flour and then coat with beaten egg. Set aside.

4 To make the crab fritters, season the crab meat with salt and pepper and place in a bowl. Add the mushrooms, pepper and chives. Then stir in the garlic, eggs and flour, and set the mixture aside.

5 To make the cod fritters, cut the fillet into bite-size pieces and season with soy sauce, white wine and sesame oil. Leave to absorb the flavours for 20 minutes. Dust the pieces of cod with flour, and coat them in beaten egg. Set them aside.

6 Coat a large frying pan with vegetable oil and place over medium heat. Add the prawn and cod fritters, with spoonfuls of the crab mixture.

7 Sauté until lightly brown and then add a little of the mushroom mixture to each prawn fritter. When all the fritters are golden brown on each side transfer them to a large serving platter.

Per portion Energy 294kcal/1227kJ; Protein 29.3g; Carbohydrate 9.1g, of which sugars 6.1g; Fat 15.3g, of which saturates 2.8g; Cholesterol 287mg; Calcium 103mg; Fibre 1.1g; Sodium 671mg.

 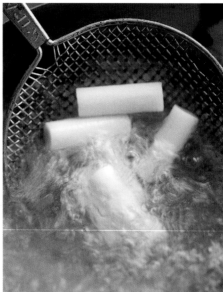 

Stir-fried rice cake with vegetables

1 long Korean rice cake
5ml/1 tsp sesame oil
2 dried shiitake mushrooms,
  soaked in warm water
  for about 30 minutes
  until softened
50g/2oz carrot
¼ cucumber
50g/2oz beef, thinly sliced
30ml/2 tbsp vegetable oil
¼ onion, finely sliced

For the seasoning
60ml/4 tbsp dark soy sauce
15ml/1 tbsp sugar
2.5ml/½ tsp ground
  white pepper
5ml/1 tsp sesame seeds
15ml/1 tbsp sesame oil
2 spring onions (scallions),
  finely chopped
30ml/2 tbsp mirin or rice wine
2 garlic cloves, crushed

Per portion Energy 369kcal/1538kJ; Protein
10.2g; Carbohydrate 35.3g, of which sugars
14.4g; Fat 21.9g, of which saturates 3.6g;
Cholesterol 15mg; Calcium 50mg; Fibre 1.5g;
Sodium 1806mg.

Hearty Korean rice cake is a versatile ingredient used in many different recipes. In *tuckboki* the sticky texture of the rice cake is complemented by the crunch of vegetables and a rich taste of beef. The refined flavour of the soy and sesame dressing harks back to this dish's origin as a royal court snack. A bowl of clear soup makes an excellent accompaniment to this quick and easy recipe. **Serves 2**

1 Slice the rice cake into 4cm/1½in lengths and blanch in salted boiling water for 2 seconds. Drain and rinse in cold water, then coat with sesame oil and set aside.

2 When the soaked shiitake mushrooms have reconstituted and become soft, drain and thinly slice them, discarding the stem.

3 Cut the carrot into thin julienne strips. Seed the cucumber and cut into thin julienne strips.

4 Combine the soy sauce, sugar, pepper, sesame seeds and oil for the seasoning in a bowl. Add the beef, coating it well with the seasoning. Leave to absorb the flavours for 15 minutes.

5 Combine the spring onions with the mirin or rice wine and crushed garlic in a small bowl.

6 Coat a frying pan or wok with the vegetable oil and place over medium heat. When the pan is hot add the onion and seasoned beef. Stir-fry until the beef is browned and then add the mushrooms, rice cake, carrot and cucumber.

7 Once the vegetables have softened slightly pour in the spring onion mixture. Reduce the heat and cook until the liquid has formed a sticky glaze over the ingredients. Transfer to a shallow serving dish and serve.

Spicy *tuckboki* For a classic spicy version of *tuckboki* try adding *gochujang* chilli paste to the seasoning instead of soy sauce, and omit the mushrooms.

Steamed tofu & chive dumplings

30 dumpling skins
1 egg, beaten

For the filling
3 spring onions (scallions),
 finely chopped
3 garlic cloves, crushed
5ml/1 tsp finely grated fresh
 root ginger
5ml/1 tsp mirin or rice wine
90g/3½oz/scant ½ cup minced
 (ground) beef
90g/3½oz firm tofu
90g/3½oz Korean chives, finely
 chopped
½ onion, finely chopped
30ml/2 tbsp soy sauce
30ml/2 tbsp sesame oil
15ml/1 tbsp sugar
15ml/1 tbsp salt
10ml/2 tsp ground black
 pepper

For the dipping sauce
60ml/4 tbsp dark soy sauce
30ml/2 tbsp rice vinegar
5ml/1 tsp Korean chilli powder

Per portion Energy 235kcal/982kJ; Protein
9.9g; Carbohydrate 26.1g, of which sugars
6.5g; Fat 10.8g, of which saturates 2.5g;
Cholesterol 14mg; Calcium 208mg; Fibre
2.2g; Sodium 1054mg.

The slight spiciness and delicate texture of Korean chives make them a wonderful
ingredient to add to these stuffed paper-thin steamed dumplings, called *mandu*.
Here the succulent filling is tofu is combined with beef and rice wine. **Serves 4**

1 To make the dipping sauce, mix the soy
sauce, rice vinegar and chilli powder in a small
serving bowl.

2 To make the filling, put the chopped spring
onions, garlic, grated ginger, mirin or rice wine
and minced beef into a large bowl and mix well.
Leave to marinate for 15 minutes.

3 Meanwhile, drain off any excess liquid from
the tofu then crumble it into a bowl. Add the
chopped chives to the seasoned beef, with
the tofu and remaining filling ingredients. Mix
together thoroughly.

4 Take a dumpling skin and brush with a little
beaten egg. Place a spoonful of the stuffing
in the middle and fold into a half-moon shape,
crimping the edges firmly to seal. Repeat with
the other dumpling skins. Place them in a
steamer over a pan of boiling water and
cook for 6 minutes. Alternatively cook the
dumplings in boiling water for 3 minutes.
Arrange on a serving dish and serve with
the soy dipping sauce.

Alternative fillings Almost any ingredient
can be adapted for *mandu* fillings: beansprouts,
minced (ground) pork, chopped prawns
(shrimp), courgettes (zucchini) and cabbage
kimchi (see page 143) are favourites.

Dumpling skins Asian stores often stock
these, which is ideal for a quick dish, but you
can make your own. For 8 dumpling skins, sift
115g/4oz/1 cup plain (all-purpose) flour and
30ml/2 tbsp cornflour (cornstarch) together in a
bowl and add 2.5ml/½ tsp salt. Pour in 50ml/
2fl oz/¼ cup warm water and knead well until it
has formed a smooth, elastic dough. Cover the
bowl with a damp dish towel and leave for 10
minutes. Place on a lightly floured surface and roll
out the dough until paper-thin. Use a floured
pastry (cookie) cutter or sharp knife to cut the
dough into circles roughly 7.5cm/3in in diameter.

Cooking dumplings Dumplings can be
cooked in a variety of ways. Steaming is the most
popular, but grilling (broiling) and shallow-frying
until golden brown also produce delicious results.

Mung bean soufflé pancakes

These mung bean pancakes, called *bindaetuk*, are deliciously light, filled with a mouth-watering combination of meat and vegetables. The flavours of rice wine and garlic in the marinade are complemented by the sharpness of the soy and vinegar in the dipping sauce. **Serves 3–4**

375g/13oz/2 cups mung beans, soaked overnight in cold water
15ml/1 tbsp pine nuts
30ml/2 tbsp sweet rice flour
75g/3oz beef flank, sliced
200g/7oz prawns (shrimp), peeled and finely chopped
15ml/1 tbsp vegetable oil, plus extra for shallow-frying
1 button (white) mushroom, thinly sliced
½ onion, thinly sliced
½ cucumber, seeded and sliced
½ cup cabbage *kimchi* (see page 143), thinly sliced
3 spring onions (scallions), thinly sliced
1 red chilli, shredded
salt and ground black pepper

For the marinade
5ml/1 tsp mirin or rice wine
2.5ml/½ tsp grated fresh root ginger
5ml/1 tsp dark soy sauce
1 garlic clove, crushed
2.5ml/½ tsp sesame seeds
5ml/1 tsp sesame oil
ground black pepper

For the dipping sauce
60ml/4 tbsp dark soy sauce
10ml/2 tsp rice vinegar
1 spring onion (scallion), finely chopped

1 Drain the mung beans and roll them between the palms of your hands to remove the skins. Rinse thoroughly, and place the peeled beans in a food processor with the pine nuts and 120ml/4fl oz/½ cup water. Blend well until they have formed a milky paste.

2 Transfer the bean paste to a bowl and add the rice flour and 5ml/1 tsp salt. Mix well.

3 Put the beef into a large bowl. Pour over the mirin or rice wine for the marinade, then add the other marinade ingredients and mix well. Leave to marinate for 20 minutes. Season the prawns with salt and pepper.

4 Combine all the dipping sauce ingredients in a small serving bowl. Coat a frying pan or wok with vegetable oil and heat over medium heat.

5 Add the beef, mushroom and onion, and stir-fry until the meat has browned. Next, add the cucumber, cabbage *kimchi* and spring onions. Toss the ingredients in the pan and then remove from the heat.

6 Heat a little oil for shallow-frying in a frying pan and add a spoonful of the bean paste to form a small pancake. Spoon a little of the beef mixture on to the pancake, with some shredded chilli and a spoonful of chopped prawns. Use a metal spatula to press the mixture flat on to the pancake, and fry until golden on each side. Repeat until all the batter and beef mixture has been used up. Arrange the pancake fritters on a large serving platter and serve with the soy dipping sauce.

Per portion Energy 492kcal/2070kJ; Protein 38.2g; Carbohydrate 55.4g, of which sugars 6.9g; Fat 14.2g, of which saturates 2.2g; Cholesterol 108mg; Calcium 175mg; Fibre 11.7g; Sodium 1867mg.

Light and delicate or rich and hearty

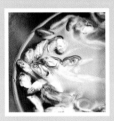 Korean soups are delicate broths, traditionally based on *doenjang* soybean paste and similar to the miso soup eaten by the Japanese. These light, clear soups often have their essence in the subtle flavours of seaweed or the more distinctively pungent white radish, and soups are generally simmered slowly. This slow cooking process allows the various different flavours of the dish to mingle and intensify, creating a product that is distinctively Korean in aroma and taste. Soups filled with staple Korean ingredients such as beansprouts and dumplings are always on the menu, but other more tempting combinations of seafood and vegetables are also popular, with deliciously chewy octopus and peppery watercress creating an exotic soup that is quintessentially Korean.

While most classic Korean soups are light and refreshing, some recipes rely on meat or fish to produce a thicker, heartier soup. These robust, flavoursome creations are perfectly suited to chilly weather, with classic dishes like hot and spicy fish soup proving a real favourite when the temperature drops below freezing. Warming, substantial soups made from chicken or mushrooms and laden with noodles are also popular once the icy winter has truly set in.

By contrast, during the summer months Koreans enjoy a number of stimulating soups to combat the scorching sunshine. Chilled soups are popular, especially the refreshing beef broth with buckwheat noodles, but no soup is more widely enjoyed on a sun-drenched afternoon than the ever popular *samgyetang*. This medley of chicken, ginseng and red dates creates a fortifying and revitalizing broth that is considered the perfect dish on the hottest of days.

Most soup dishes are accompanied by a bowl of rice, although it is not unusual to have the rice already in the soup when it is served. Despite creating a thicker, more substantial soup this should not be confused with the heartier *chungol* stews that also adorn the Korean dinner table. Soups are an integral part of every Korean meal, and each person dining will invariably have a bowl of their own, while stews are more lavish dishes and will traditionally be served in the centre of the table where they can be shared.

Garnishes are simple, normally limited to just shredded spring onions (scallions) or chopped garlic, and soups are seasoned sparingly, relying instead on the natural saltiness of the stock to add zest. One common addition to any bowl of soup, however, is a beaten egg. Poured slowly into the steaming liquid this will form wisps of poached egg in the bowl, and adds a delicious combination of flavour and texture.

Designed to be refreshing in the summer and fortifying in the winter, Korean soups can be enjoyed as part of a lavish repast, or alternatively eaten simply with rice and *kimchi* (see page 143) as a light and delicious meal.

Spinach & clam soup

The leafy flavour of the fresh spinach marries perfectly with the nutty taste of the *doenjang* soybean paste to make this delicious soup with clams. **Serves 3**

9 clams
90g/3½oz spinach
2 spring onions (scallions)
40g/1½oz/scant ¼ cup minced (ground) beef

15ml/1 tbsp *doenjang* soybean paste
15ml/1 tbsp crushed garlic
salt

1 Scrub the clams in cold running water, and rinse the spinach. Cut the spring onions lengthways and then into 5cm/2in strips.

2 Place the minced beef and soybean paste in a pan, and stir over medium heat until the beef is well cooked. Pour in 750ml/1¼ pints/ 3 cups water, cover, bring to the boil and add the clams and spinach.

3 Once the clams have opened, add the spring onions and garlic. Discard any clams that remain closed. Add salt to taste, and serve.

Variations
• For a vegetarian alternative use vegetable stock in place of the minced beef, and substitute tofu for the clams.

Per portion Energy 90kcal/377kJ; Protein 11.1g; Carbohydrate 4.7g, of which sugars 3.8g; Fat 3.1g, of which saturates 1.1g; Cholesterol 30mg; Calcium 119mg; Fibre 2.2g; Sodium 1471mg.

Seaweed soup

This rich Korean broth is packed with silky green ribbons of seaweed. Seaweed soup is said to detoxify the body and help the circulation. A chilled version can be served as a summer side dish. **Serves 4**

25g/1oz dried seaweed
40g/1½oz beef, diced
37.5ml/7½ tsp sesame oil
3 garlic cloves, finely chopped

45ml/3 tbsp light soy sauce
salt and ground black pepper

1 Soak the dried seaweed for about 20 minutes, or until softened. Drain and cut into 2.5cm/1in lengths.

2 Season the beef with 15ml/1 tbsp of the sesame oil and ground black pepper, and set aside for 10 minutes. Add the beef and seaweed to a large pan, and stir-fry using the remaining sesame oil.

3 When the meat is cooked, add 750ml/1¼ pints/3 cups water, cover and bring to the boil. Add the garlic and soy sauce. Cover and boil until it has turned slightly milky in colour. Season before serving.

Seaweed Dried seaweed can be found at Asian food stores and health food stores. This dish is best prepared with Korean *miyuk* or Japanese *wakame*.

Per portion Energy 77kcal/318kJ; Protein 2.5g; Carbohydrate 0.7g, of which sugars 0.6g; Fat 7.2g, of which saturates 1.3g; Cholesterol 6mg; Calcium 3mg; Fibre 0.1g; Sodium 274mg.

Dumpling soup

The succulent dumplings taste fantastic in this clear soup. With ready-to-eat dumplings widely available this dish is simple, and the dumpling flavours suffuse the nourishing broth. **Serves 4**

750ml/1¼ pints/3 cups beef
  stock
16 frozen dumplings
1 spring onion (scallion), sliced

¼ green chilli, sliced
1 garlic clove, crushed
15ml/1 tbsp light soy sauce
salt and ground black pepper

1 Place the beef stock in a pan and bring to the boil. Add the frozen dumplings, cover, and boil for 6 minutes.

2 Add the spring onion, chilli, garlic and soy sauce, and boil for a further 2 minutes.

3 Season with salt and black pepper, and serve piping hot.

Cook's tips
• If you want to use fresh dumplings, cook them for 5 minutes.
• Soy sauce with a drop of vinegar makes a good dipping sauce for the dumplings.
• When cooking dumplings don't stir the soup as this can often cause the dumplings to tear open.

Per portion Energy 106kcal/445kJ; Protein 2g; Carbohydrate 12.6g, of which sugars 0.6g; Fat 6.1g, of which saturates 3.4g; Cholesterol 5mg; Calcium 30mg; Fibre 0.5g; Sodium 842mg.

White radish & beef soup

The smoky flavours of the beef are perfectly complemented by the sweet tanginess of Chinese white radish in this mild and refreshing soup with a slightly sweet edge. **Serves 4**

200g/7oz Chinese white radish,
  peeled
50g/2oz beef
15ml/1 tbsp sesame oil

½ leek, sliced
15ml/1 tbsp light soy sauce
salt and ground black pepper

1 Slice the white radish, and cut the pieces into 2cm/¾in squares. Roughly chop the beef into bitesize cubes.

2 Heat the sesame oil in a large pan, and stir-fry the beef until tender and golden brown. Add the white radish, and briefly stir-fry.

3 Add 750ml/1¼ pints/3 cups water to the pan. Bring to the boil, cover and simmer for 7 minutes. Add the leek and soy sauce. Simmer for a further 2 minutes. Season to taste and serve.

Radish The long white radish, or *daikon*, is used extensively in Korean cooking and can be found at Asian stores.

Per portion Energy 60kcal/247kJ; Protein 3.7g; Carbohydrate 2g, of which sugars 1.8g; Fat 4.1g, of which saturates 1g; Cholesterol 7mg; Calcium 17mg; Fibre 1g; Sodium 281mg.

Noodle soup with oyster mushrooms

80g/3oz Julienne beef
30ml/2 tbsp light soy sauce
2 eggs, beaten
50ml/3 tbsp vegetable oil
4 oyster mushrooms
80g/3oz courgette (zucchini)
sesame oil, for drizzling
100g/4oz plain noodles
1 spring onion (scallion),
  finely chopped
1 dried red chilli, thinly sliced
2 garlic cloves, crushed
salt and ground white pepper
sesame seeds, to garnish

Colloquially known as "marketplace noodles" this dish has long been enjoyed as a quick and simple lunch. The oyster mushrooms give the mild broth an appetizing richness, while the noodles have a hint of beef and a dash of chilli. Serve the soup with an accompaniment of radish *kimchi* (see page 145) and a bowl of steamed rice. **Serves 2**

1 Pour 500ml/17fl oz/2¼ cups water into a pan and bring to the boil. Add the beef and cook until tender, about 20 minutes. Remove the meat and slice into thin strips. Strain the cooking liquid through a sieve into a jug (pitcher). Add the light soy sauce to the stock and set aside.

2 Season the beaten eggs with a pinch of salt. Coat a frying pan with 10ml/2 tsp vegetable oil and heat over medium heat. Add the beaten eggs and make a thin omelette, browning gently on each side. Remove from the pan and cut into thin strips.

3 Cut the oyster mushrooms and courgette into thin julienne strips. Sprinkle both with a little salt. Pat the courgette dry with kitchen paper after 5 minutes.

4 Coat a frying pan or wok with the remaining vegetable oil and heat over medium heat. Quickly stir-fry the mushrooms and drizzle with sesame oil before setting them aside. Next, lightly fry the courgette until it softens, then remove from the wok. Finally, stir-fry the beef until it has lightly browned, and set aside.

5 Bring a pan of water to the boil and cook the plain noodles, then drain them and rinse in cold water. Quickly reheat the reserved beef stock.

6 Place the noodles at the base of a soup dish and cover with the mushrooms, courgette and sliced beef. Top with the spring onion, chilli and garlic, then pour over the beef stock until roughly one-third of the ingredients are covered. Finally, sprinkle with sesame seeds before serving.

Per portion Energy 492kcal/2059kJ; Protein 23.1g; Carbohydrate 40.4g, of which sugars 3.3g; Fat 27.7g, of which saturates 4.9g; Cholesterol 213mg; Calcium 60mg; Fibre 2.3g; Sodium 1167mg.

Strands of thin wheat noodles taste great in a mild and deliciously nutty chilled soup, making an ideal dish for a hot summer's day. The iced broth is topped with succulent strips of cucumber and wedges of tomato. **Serves 4**

Wheat noodles in soybean soup

185g/6½oz/1 cup soya beans
30ml/2 tbsp sesame seeds
300g/11oz thin wheat noodles
salt

1 cucumber, cut into thin strips and 1 tomato, cut into wedges, to garnish

1 Soak the soya beans overnight. Rinse in cold water and then roll them between your palms to remove the skins.

2 Gently toast the sesame seeds in a dry pan until they have lightly browned. Place the peeled soya beans and the sesame seeds in a food processor. Add 1 litre/1¾ pints/4 cups water and process until fine. Strain through muslin (cheesecloth), collecting the liquid in a jug (pitcher). Chill the soya and sesame milk in the refrigerator.

3 Bring a pan of water to the boil and cook the noodles, then drain them and rinse in cold water.

4 Place a portion of noodles in each soup bowl, and pour over the chilled liquid. Garnish with strips of cucumber and tomato wedges, then season with salt and serve.

Soya milk For a quick and easy version of this dish use 250ml/8fl oz/1 cup unsweetened soya milk rather than the soaked soya beans. Simply add the ground sesame seeds to the soya milk and chill to make the soup.

Per portion Energy 268kcal/1121kJ; Protein 20.1g; Carbohydrate 17.9g, of which sugars 3.4g; Fat 13.3g, of which saturates 1.7g; Cholesterol 0mg; Calcium 174mg; Fibre 8.7g; Sodium 6mg.

This gentle broth, *kongnamul*, is easy to make and easy on the palate, with just a hint of spiciness and a refreshing nutty flavour. It is reputed to be the perfect solution for calming your stomach after a heavy drinking session. **Serves 4**

Soya beansprout soup

200g/7oz/generous 2 cups
  soya beansprouts
1 red or green chilli
15 dried anchovies

1 spring onion (scallion),
  finely sliced
3 garlic cloves, chopped
salt

1 Wash the soya beansprouts, and trim off the tail ends.

2 Seed the chilli and cut it diagonally into thin slices.

3 Boil 750ml/1¼ pints/3 cups water in a pan and add the dried anchovies. After boiling for 15 minutes remove the anchovies and discard.

4 Add the soya beansprouts and boil for 5 minutes, ensuring the lid is kept tightly on. Add the spring onion, chilli and garlic, and boil for a further 3 minutes. Add salt to taste, and serve.

Dried anchovies Soya beansprouts and dried anchovies are available at some Asian stores. If you are unable to find dried anchovies, then 5ml/1 tsp Thai fish sauce can be used instead.

Hot and spicy To make a spicier version simply add 5ml/ 1 tsp of chilli powder to each bowl – great for curing a cold!

Per portion Energy 41kcal/173kJ; Protein 4.6g; Carbohydrate 2.7g, of which sugars 1.2g; Fat 1.4g, of which saturates 0.2g; Cholesterol 7mg; Calcium 46mg; Fibre 1g; Sodium 445mg.

Spicy seafood noodle soup

50g/2oz pork loin
50g/2oz mussels
50g/2oz prawns (shrimp)
90g/3½oz squid
15ml/1 tbsp vegetable oil
1 dried chilli, sliced
½ leek, sliced
2 garlic cloves, finely sliced
5ml/1 tsp grated fresh
   root ginger
30ml/2 tbsp Korean
   chilli powder
5ml/1 tsp mirin or rice wine
50g/2oz bamboo shoots, sliced
½ onion, roughly chopped
50g/2oz carrot,
   roughly chopped
2 Chinese leaves (Chinese
   cabbage), roughly chopped
750ml/1¼ pints/3 cups
   beef stock
light soy sauce, to taste
300g/11oz udon or flat
   wheat noodles
salt

Jampong is a spicy, garlic-infused stew overflowing with squid, prawns and mussels. Thick Japanese udon noodles are added to the rich, meaty broth flavoured with characteristically Korean seasonings to create an enticing fusion dish. Add a bowl of steamed rice for the perfect quick lunch. **Serves 2**

1 Slice the pork thinly, and set aside.

2 Prepare the seafood. Scrub the mussels' shells with a stiff brush and rinse under cold running water. Discard any mussels that remain closed after being sharply tapped. Scrape off any barnacles and remove the "beards" with a small knife. Rinse well. Hold each prawn between two fingers and gently pull off the tail shell. Twist off the head. Peel away the soft body shell and the small claws beneath. Rinse well.

3 Wash the squid. Holding the body, pull away the head and tentacles. Remove and discard the ink sac, if intact. Pull out the innards including the long transparent "pen". Peel off and discard the thin purple skin, but keep the two small side fins. Slice the head across just under the eyes, severing the tentacles. Discard the rest of the head. Squeeze the tentacles at the head end to push out the round beak in the centre and discard. Rinse the pouch and tentacles. (Your fishmonger can prepare squid.) Score the flesh in a crisscross pattern, and slice into 2cm/¾in pieces.

4 Coat a heavy pan with the vegetable oil and place over high heat. Add the chilli, leek, garlic and ginger. Stir-fry until the garlic has lightly browned and add the sliced pork. Stir-fry quickly, add the chilli powder and mirin or rice wine, and coat the ingredients well.

5 Add the bamboo shoots, onion and carrot, and stir-fry until the vegetables have softened.

6 Add the seafood and cabbage and cook over high heat for 30 seconds. Pour in the beef stock and bring to the boil. Reduce the heat. Season with salt and soy sauce, then cover and simmer for 3 minutes. Discard any closed mussels.

7 Cook the udon or wheat noodles in a pan of boiling water until soft, then drain and rinse with cold water. Place a portion of noodles in each soup bowl, ladle over the soup and serve.

Variations Pak choi (bok choy) can replace the Chinese leaves (Chinese cabbage), and chilli oil the chilli powder.

Per portion Energy 778kcal/3288kJ; Protein 39.5g; Carbohydrate 122.8g, of which sugars 9.4g; Fat 17.7g, of which saturates 1.4g; Cholesterol 176mg; Calcium 104mg; Fibre 6.9g; Sodium 734mg.

This refreshing seafood soup has a wonderfully restorative quality. Delicious octopus is cooked in a rich vegetable broth, with white radish and watercress adding an elusive flavour that is quintessentially Korean.
Serves 2–3

Octopus & watercress soup

1 large octopus, cleaned and gutted
150g/5oz Chinese white radish, peeled
½ leek, sliced
20g/¾oz kelp or spinach leaves

3 garlic cloves, crushed
1 red chilli, seeded and sliced
15ml/1 tbsp light soy sauce
75g/3oz watercress or rocket (arugula)
salt and ground black pepper

1 Rinse the octopus in salted water and cut into pieces about 2.5cm/1in long. Finely dice the white radish.

2 Pour 750ml/1¼ pints/3 cups water into a large pan and bring to the boil. Reduce the heat and add the radish, leek, kelp or spinach, and crushed garlic. Simmer over medium heat until the radish softens and becomes clear. Discard the kelp and leek and then add the sliced chilli.

3 Add the octopus, increase the heat and boil for 5 minutes. Season with soy sauce, salt and pepper, and then add the watercress or rocket. Remove from the heat, cover the pan and leave to stand for 1 minute while the leaves wilt into the liquid. Ladle into bowls and serve.

Variation For a spicier version of this soup try adding a teaspoon of Korean chilli powder. This gives the dish a really tangy kick!

Per portion Energy 106kcal/449kJ; Protein 19.9g; Carbohydrate 2.6g, of which sugars 2.3g; Fat 1.9g, of which saturates 0.5g; Cholesterol 48mg; Calcium 108mg; Fibre 1.7g; Sodium 386mg.

This soup is a firm favourite to accompany a glass of *soju*, and has a delicious spicy kick. Halibut or sea bass work as well as cod. The white fish flakes have the bite of red chilli, and the watercress and spring onions add a refreshing zesty quality. **Serves 3–4**

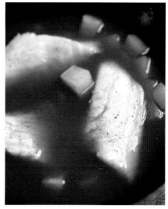

Hot & spicy fish soup

1 cod, filleted and skinned, head separate
225g/8oz Chinese white radish, peeled
½ onion, chopped
2 garlic cloves, crushed
22.5ml/4½ tsp Korean chilli powder
5ml/1 tsp *gochujang* chilli paste
2 spring onions (scallions), roughly sliced
1 block firm tofu, cubed
90g/3½oz watercress or rocket (arugula)
salt and ground black pepper

1 Slice the cod fillets into three or four large pieces and set the head aside. Cut the white radish into 2cm/¾in cubes.

2 Bring 750ml/1¼ pints/3 cups water to the boil in large pan, and add the fish head. Add the radish, onion, crushed garlic and a pinch of salt. Then add the chilli powder and *gochujang* chilli paste, and boil for 5 minutes more.

3 Remove the fish head and add the sliced fillet to the pan. Simmer until the fish is tender, about 4 minutes, and then add the spring onions, tofu, and watercress or rocket. Simmer the soup without stirring for 2 minutes more.

4 Season with salt and pepper, and serve the soup immediately.

Mild fish soup For a milder version omit the chilli powder and *gochujang* chilli paste. The soup will still be wonderfully hearty and flavoursome.

Per portion Energy 132kcal/554kJ; Protein 23.4g; Carbohydrate 2.8g, of which sugars 2.3g; Fat 3g, of which saturates 0.5g; Cholesterol 46mg; Calcium 300mg; Fibre 1.1g; Sodium 80mg.

Chicken soup with hand-made noodles

The hand-made wheat noodles are impressive in this dish, although they are remarkably easy to make. The noodles are bathed in a hot chicken broth and topped with julienne vegetables, seasoned chicken shreds and a dash of spicy sauce. **Serves 2**

1 Roughly slice the chicken into large pieces and place in a large pan. Add the leeks, garlic and root ginger, and cover the ingredients with water. Bring to the boil over medium heat, and boil for 20 minutes, or until the chicken is tender. Remove the chicken and strain the cooking liquid into a jug (pitcher).

2 Skin and bone the chicken, and tear the meat into thin strips. Mix the seasoning ingredients in a large bowl with a pinch of salt and ground white pepper. Add the chicken strips, coat them with the seasoning, and set aside to absorb the flavours.

3 Meanwhile, prepare the noodles. Sift the plain flour into a large bowl with a pinch of salt, and add the beaten eggs and a splash of water. Mix together thoroughly by hand, and knead the dough until it is smooth and elastic. Place on a lightly floured surface, and roll out the dough to about 3mm/⅛in thick. The dough will be firm and slightly sticky to the touch. Fold it three times and then, using a sharp knife, slice it into thin noodles.

4 When the soaked shiitake mushrooms have reconstituted and become soft, drain and slice them, discarding the stems. Cut the carrot and courgette into thin julienne strips.

5 Heat the vegetable oil in a frying pan over medium heat and lightly stir-fry the mushrooms, courgette, carrot and onion. Season with the sesame oil and a pinch of salt, and then set aside.

6 Combine all the sauce ingredients in a small dish, adding a little water if the mixture is too dry.

7 Heat the reserved chicken stock in a large pan and season with the light soy sauce, salt and pepper. Once it is boiling add the noodles and cook for 4 minutes. Transfer the cooked noodles to a serving bowl and ladle the chicken broth over the top. Top with the shredded chicken, julienne vegetables and a sprinkling of dried chilli. Serve with the sauce, to stir into the soup before eating.

Getting the balance right When serving, pour in roughly a third more soup than noodles for just the right balance of flavours.

½ whole chicken, about 500g/1¼lb
2 leeks
4 garlic cloves, peeled
40g/1½oz fresh root ginger, peeled
8 dried shiitake mushrooms, soaked in warm water for about 30 minutes until softened
100g/4oz carrot
1 courgette (zucchini)
30ml/2 tbsp vegetable oil
1 onion, finely chopped
10ml/2 tsp sesame oil
light soy sauce, to taste
½ dried chilli, finely chopped
salt and ground white pepper

For the seasoning
10ml/2 tsp dark soy sauce
2 spring onions (scallions), finely chopped
2 garlic cloves, crushed
30ml/2 tbsp sesame oil
30ml/2 tbsp sesame seeds

For the noodles
225g/8oz/2 cups plain (all-purpose) flour
6 eggs, beaten

For the sauce
30ml/2 tbsp light soy sauce
2 spring onions (scallions), finely chopped
2 garlic cloves, crushed
10ml/2 tsp Korean chilli powder
10ml/2 tsp sesame seeds
15ml/1 tbsp sesame oil

Per portion Energy 1138kcal/4767kJ; Protein 94.1g; Carbohydrate 70.4g, of which sugars 11.4g; Fat 55.6g, of which saturates 10.5g; Cholesterol 746mg; Calcium 392mg; Fibre 10.1g; Sodium 739mg.

Traditionally eaten on the hottest day of summer, *samgyetang* is a smooth chicken broth with a revitalizing quality. The combination of red dates and ginseng simmering with the chicken provides a unique flavour, and makes a genuinely memorable dish. *Samgyetang* is traditionally served with a small dish of salt and ground pepper, which can be used to season the chicken while eating. **Serves 2**

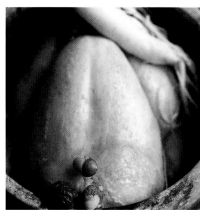

Summer soup with ginseng & red dates

180g/7oz/1 cup short grain or pudding rice
800g/1¾lb whole small chicken or poussin
4 chestnuts, peeled
4 garlic cloves, peeled

2 red dates
2 fresh ginseng roots
4 gingko nuts
salt and ground black pepper
finely shredded spring onions (scallions), to garnish

1 Soak the rice in a bowl of cold water for 20 minutes. Meanwhile, remove the wing tips and neck from the chicken, clean it thoroughly and sprinkle with salt.

2 Drain the rice and combine with the chestnuts and garlic to make a stuffing. Pack the stuffing into the neck end of the body cavity and pull down the skin before trussing the chicken.

3 Place the stuffed chicken into a heavy pan and add enough cold water to cover. Bring to the boil.

4 Once the water is boiling add the red dates, ginseng roots and gingko nuts. Reduce the heat and simmer the soup for 1 hour, or until it thickens.

5 Transfer to a bowl and serve garnished with spring onions.

Per portion Energy 630kcal/2654kJ; Protein 56.3g; Carbohydrate 93.1g, of which sugars 12.3g; Fat 3.6g, of which saturates 0.8g; Cholesterol 140mg; Calcium 60mg; Fibre 2.2g; Sodium 128mg.

Yukgejang is one of the most traditional Korean soups. The smoky taste of fern fronds gives it its unique flavour, and red chilli powder provides a fierce kick and fiery colour to the combination of beef and leek. *Yukgejang* makes a perfect lunch dish when served with a bowl of rice and accompanied by *kimchi* (see page 143). **Serves 2–3**

Hot & spicy beef soup

75g/3oz dried fern fronds
75g/3oz enoki mushrooms, trimmed
250g/9oz beef flank
10ml/2 tsp sesame oil
30ml/2 tbsp chilli powder
1 garlic clove, finely chopped
15ml/1 tbsp vegetable oil
75g/3oz/½ cup beansprouts, trimmed
1 leek, sliced
1 spring onion (scallion), sliced
salt

1 Boil the dried fern fronds for about 3 minutes. Drain and rinse with cold water. Cut the fronds into thirds, and discard the tougher stem pieces, along with the enoki mushroom caps.

2 Place the beef in a medium pan and cover with water. Bring to the boil, cover and cook over high heat for 30 minutes. Then remove the beef and strain the stock into a jug (pitcher).

3 Cut the beef into thin strips and place in a bowl. Add the sesame oil, chilli powder and chopped garlic, and coat the meat.

4 Heat the vegetable oil in a large pan and add the meat with the fern fronds, beansprouts, leek and spring onion. Stir-fry for 2 minutes, then reduce the heat and pour in the beef stock. Cover and cook over medium heat for 30 minutes or so until tender.

5 Add the enoki mushrooms and simmer for a further 2 minutes. Add salt to taste and serve.

Fern fronds If ferns are not available the best alternative is an equivalent amount of shiitake mushrooms.

Per portion Energy 225kcal/935kJ; Protein 21.5g; Carbohydrate 3g, of which sugars 2g; Fat 14.1g, of which saturates 4g; Cholesterol 48mg; Calcium 28mg; Fibre 2.3g; Sodium 59mg.

Beef broth with buckwheat noodles

90g/3½oz beef shank
1 leek, roughly chopped
½ onion, peeled and roughly
  chopped
10g/¼oz fresh root ginger,
  peeled and roughly chopped
4 garlic cloves, peeled and
  chopped
1 hard-boiled egg
¼ Chinese white radish, peeled
½ cucumber
1 Asian pear
90g/3½oz *naengmyun*
  buckwheat noodles
ice cubes, to serve

For the seasoning
15ml/1 tbsp rice vinegar
15ml/1 tbsp sugar
ready-made English (hot)
  mustard, sugar, rice vinegar
  and salt, for seasoning at
  the table

Per portion Energy 403kcal/1698kJ; Protein
22.2g; Carbohydrate 57.5g, of which sugars
22.9g; Fat 10.9g, of which saturates 2.8g;
Cholesterol 131mg; Calcium 100mg; Fibre
6.8g; Sodium 87mg.

The refreshing properties of this wonderful chilled broth, *naengmyun*, make it a perennially popular dish in the heat of summer. The buckwheat noodles float in a traditional soup which is distinctly flavoured by mustard and rice vinegar, and topped with matchsticks of crunchy Chinese radish. **Serves 2**

1 Place the beef in a large bowl of cold water. Leave it to soak for 30 minutes, then drain.

2 Pour 1 litre/1¾ pints/4 cups water into a large pan and bring to the boil. Add the beef and reduce the heat. Simmer for 1 hour, skimming the fat and foam from the surface throughout. Add the leek, onion, root ginger and garlic, and cook for another 20 minutes. Remove the meat and cut it into thin slices.

3 Strain the soup through a sieve into a jug (pitcher). Cool and chill in the refrigerator. Slice the hard-boiled egg in half. Cut the radish into thin julienne strips. Seed the cucumber and cut into thin julienne strips. Peel and core the Asian pear and cut it into thin julienne strips.

4 Place the radish strips in a bowl and add the rice vinegar and sugar and a pinch of salt. Coat the radish and leave to chill.

5 Prepare a large pan of boiling water, and cook the noodles for 5 minutes. Drain and rinse two or three times in cold water until the water runs clear. Chill in the refrigerator.

6 Pour the chilled broth into two individual serving bowls, adding a couple of ice cubes to each. Add a portion of noodles and divide the sliced beef, pear, cucumber and seasoned radish between them both. Top with half an egg.

7 Place the mustard, sugar, rice vinegar and salt in small serving dishes and serve with the soup for seasoning at the table. Stir the seasonings into the broth, according to taste, while you eat. Start with 5ml/1 tsp of vinegar and 2.5ml/½ tsp mustard, with a pinch of salt and sugar.

Succulent velvet textures and crispy smokiness

 The Korean kitchen has created many methods of seasoning and cooking poultry, taking advantage of the fact that the taste marries as well with sweet flavours as it does with spicy ones. Deep-fried chicken dishes have become more popular in recent times, but the traditional methods of griddling and stewing still retain a firm place in the hearts of the people.

Although chicken is eaten less frequently than other types of meat on the Korean peninsula, its milder flavour and velvet texture make it a popular basis for a range of dishes. The piquancy of sweet and spicy chicken is mellowed by a sugary glaze of pineapple and maple syrup, and makes for a deliciously crispy dish, while chilli-marinated chicken cooked on the barbecue is a wonderfully tangy treat, with hints of garlic sweetness.

Historically, because pork was relatively cheap in comparison to other meat and poultry it became a popular option, and this has continued right up to the present day. Pork dishes are usually prepared either by charcoal griddling or by boiling, and are accompanied by fresh vegetables to balance the flavours.

The most popular dishes use pork belly – thinly sliced, griddled and wrapped in green leaves – to meld a crispy smokiness with a refreshing succulence. The common trait among Korean pork dishes is a delectable saltiness that makes them irresistible, and the perfect companion to a glass of *soju*.

As with other Asian cuisine the addictive combination of sweet and sour is popular in Korean cooking, although it has a much subtler taste than its Chinese counterpart. The classic Korean recipe combines tender, stir-fried golden pork with ginger and crunchy sweet peppers in a delightfully sticky sauce to create a wonderfully tempting dish. Poached pork in green leaves is another national favourite, imbued with flavours of bean paste and garlic. This dish incorporates a zesty radish stuffing with the meltingly tender meat, wrapped in Chinese leaves to create a blend of tastes and textures that are both unfamiliar and unforgettable.

Tempting hearty chicken stews are simmered on autumn evenings with fiercely spicy chillies imparting a warm and homely flavour to the dish, while the copious amounts of *gochujang* chilli paste added to pork dishes set the taste of the meltingly tender meat ablaze. These two enticing flavours provide a matchless foundation for dishes that evoke the very soul of Korean cuisine.

Sweet & spicy chicken

This deep-fried chicken dish has a spicy kick, mellowed by the sweetness of pineapple and maple syrup. The crisp golden exterior envelops the soft texture of the meat, and the heat of the chilli and garlic lends a real sharpness to the taste. **Serves 3**

1 Slice the chicken into bitesize strips and season with the salt and pepper.

2 Combine all the marinade ingredients in a large bowl. Mix well and add the chicken, rubbing the mixture thoroughly into the meat. Leave to marinate for 20 minutes.

3 Sprinkle the marinated chicken with a thin coating of cornflour, making sure to cover the meat evenly. Fill a wok or medium heavy pan one-third full of vegetable oil and heat over high heat to 170°C/340°F, or when a small piece of bread dropped into the oil browns in 15 seconds.

4 Add the chicken and deep-fry for 3–5 minutes, or until golden brown. Remove the chicken and drain on kitchen paper to remove any excess oil.

5 Blend all the sauce ingredients together in a large pan, adding the garlic cloves whole, and heat over medium heat.

6 Once the sauce is bubbling, add the fried chicken and stir to coat the meat with the sauce. Leave to simmer until the sauce has formed a sticky glaze over the chicken, and then add the chillies. Stir well and transfer to a shallow serving dish. Garnish with the walnuts before serving.

Variation For a milder version of this dish try replacing the chilli oil and *gochujang* chilli paste with a squeeze of lemon juice.

675g/1½lb chicken breast fillets or boneless thighs
175g/6oz/1½ cups cornflour (cornstarch)
vegetable oil, for deep-frying
2 green chillies, sliced
2 dried red chillies, seeded and sliced
3 walnuts, finely chopped
salt and ground black pepper

For the marinade
15ml/1 tbsp white wine
15ml/1 tbsp dark soy sauce
3 garlic cloves, crushed
¼ onion, finely chopped

For the sauce
15ml/1 tbsp chilli oil
2.5ml/½ tsp *gochujang* chilli paste
30ml/2 tbsp dark soy sauce
7.5ml/1½ tsp pineapple juice
15 garlic cloves, peeled
30ml/2 tbsp maple syrup
15ml/1 tbsp sugar

Per portion Energy 655kcal/2749kJ; Protein 56.4g; Carbohydrate 45.3g, of which sugars 14.4g; Fat 28.8g, of which saturates 3.5g; Cholesterol 158mg; Calcium 34mg; Fibre 0.4g; Sodium 1249mg.

Hot, spicy, garlicky and a little sweet, this is a truly tasty dish. Griddled so it cooks faster than the slow-smoked variety, it has the same delicious scorched flavour. Stuffed cucumber *kimchi* (see page 144) makes a refreshing accompaniment. **Serves 4**

Chicken marinated in chilli paste

900g/2lb chicken breast fillet or boneless thighs
2 round (butterhead) lettuces
vegetable oil
4 spring onions (scallions), shredded

For the marinade
60ml/4 tbsp *gochujang* chilli paste

45ml/3 tbsp mirin or rice wine
15ml/1 tbsp dark soy sauce
4 garlic cloves, crushed
25ml/5 tsp sesame oil
15ml/1 tbsp grated fresh root ginger
2 spring onions (scallions), finely chopped
10ml/2 tsp ground black pepper
15ml/1 tbsp lemonade

1 Combine all the marinade ingredients in a large bowl.

2 Cut the chicken into bitesize pieces, add to the bowl and stir to coat it with the marinade. Transfer to an airtight container and marinate in the refrigerator for about 3 hours.

3 Remove the outer leaves from the heads of lettuce, keeping them whole. Rinse well and place in a serving dish.

4 Lightly coat a heavy griddle pan or frying pan with vegetable oil and place it over medium heat (the griddle can be used over charcoal). Griddle the chicken for 15 minutes, or until the meat is cooked and has turned a deep brown. Increase the heat briefly to scorch the chicken and give it a smoky flavour.

5 Serve by wrapping the chicken pieces in lettuce leaves with a few shredded spring onions.

Per portion Energy 279kcal/1178kJ; Protein 55g; Carbohydrate 2g, of which sugars 2g; Fat 5.7g, of which saturates 1.1g; Cholesterol 158mg; Calcium 39mg; Fibre 0.9g; Sodium 405mg.

This dish, a favourite of the Korean royal court, smothers tender chicken in a rich mushroom sauce. Strips of poultry are coated with a sticky glaze that blends woodland flavours with soy sauce and ginger. Serve with rice, soup and *kimchi* (see page 143). **Serves 2**

Chicken with soy dressing

1 leek, roughly sliced
10ml/2 tsp chopped fresh
 root ginger
300g/10oz chicken breast fillet
10ml/2 tsp sesame oil, plus
 extra for drizzling
salt and ground black pepper

For the sauce
6 dried shiitake mushrooms,
 soaked in warm water for
 about 30 minutes

30ml/2 tbsp vegetable oil
1 garlic clove, finely chopped
10 oyster mushrooms, sliced
30ml/2 tbsp dark soy sauce
60ml/4 tbsp maple syrup
30ml/2 tbsp plain
 (all-purpose) flour
2 eggs, beaten
salt and ground black
 pepper

1 Place the leek, root ginger and chicken in a pan, cover with water and bring to the boil. After 5 minutes remove the chicken from the water. Strain the liquid into a measuring jug (cup).

2 When the soaked shiitake mushrooms have reconstituted and become soft, drain and slice them, discarding the stems. Tear the cooked chicken into strips and add salt, pepper and sesame oil.

3 Stir-fry the garlic in the vegetable oil and add the mushrooms and soy sauce. Sauté for a few minutes and pour in 300ml/½ pint/1¼ cups of stock. Add the maple syrup and stir.

4 Bring the sauce to the boil, add the flour and simmer, stirring until the sauce thickens. Add the beaten egg, gently poaching it.

5 Place the strips of chicken on a serving platter, pour over the mushroom sauce and drizzle with sesame oil.

Per portion Energy 567kcal/2381kJ; Protein 47.2g; Carbohydrate 39.7g, of which sugars 27.3g; Fat 25.6g, of which saturates 4.5g; Cholesterol 314mg; Calcium 95mg; Fibre 3.2g; Sodium 1321mg.

Gochujang chicken stew

Dakdoritang is a warming autumn stew filled with vegetables and spices to ward off the cold. Chillies and *gochujang* chilli paste supply a vivid red colour and give the chicken a fiery quality. With a delicious hint of sweetness offsetting the piquancy, this is the perfect hearty meal for chilly evenings. Keep accompanying dishes simple, ideally just steamed rice and a mild *namul* dish. **Serves 4**

1 Peel the potatoes and cut into bitesize pieces. Soak in cold water for 15–20 minutes and drain. Peel the carrot and onions and cut into medium-size pieces.

2 Cut the chicken, with skin and bone, into bitesize pieces and place in a dish with the marinade ingredients. Stir to coat and leave for 10 minutes.

3 Heat 15ml/1 tbsp vegetable oil in a frying pan or wok, and quickly stir-fry the crushed garlic. Add the chicken and stir-fry, draining off any fat that comes from the meat during cooking. When lightly browned, place the chicken on kitchen paper to remove any excess oil.

4 To make the seasoning, grind the sesame seeds in a mortar and pestle. Combine the soy sauce, *gochujang* paste, chilli powder and ground sesame seeds in a bowl.

5 In a pan heat the remaining vegetable oil and add the potatoes, carrot and onions. Briefly cook over medium heat, stirring well, and then add the chicken.

6 Pour over enough water so that two-thirds of the meat and vegetables are immersed, and bring to the boil. Add the chilli seasoning and reduce the heat. Stir the seasoning into the water and simmer until the volume of liquid has reduced by about one-third.

7 Add the sliced chillies and simmer for a little longer until the liquid has thickened slightly.

8 Add the sesame oil, transfer to deep serving bowls and garnish with the chopped spring onion before serving.

3 potatoes
1 carrot
2 onions
1 chicken, about 800g/1¾lb
30ml/2 tbsp vegetable oil
2 garlic cloves, crushed
3 green chillies, seeded and finely sliced
1 red chilli, seeded and finely sliced
15ml/1 tbsp sesame oil
salt and ground black pepper
2 spring onions (scallions), finely chopped, to garnish

For the marinade
30ml/2 tbsp mirin or rice wine
salt and ground black pepper

For the seasoning
15ml/1 tbsp sesame seeds
10ml/2 tsp light soy sauce
30ml/2 tbsp *gochujang* chilli paste
45ml/3 tbsp Korean chilli powder

Per portion Energy 470kcal/1955kJ; Protein 27.4g; Carbohydrate 20.4g, of which sugars 4.7g; Fat 31.5g, of which saturates 7.5g; Cholesterol 128mg; Calcium 56mg; Fibre 2.3g; Sodium 296mg.

1 head Chinese leaves (Chinese cabbage)
5 garlic cloves, roughly chopped
½ onion, roughly chopped
1 leek, roughly chopped
15ml/1 tbsp *doenjang* soybean paste
100ml/3½fl oz/scant ½ cup sake or rice wine
675g/1½lb pork neck
salt
sugar

For the stuffing
500g/1¼lb Chinese white radish, peeled and thinly sliced
3 chestnuts, sliced
½ Asian pear, sliced
65g/2½oz *minari*, watercress, or rocket (arugula), chopped
45ml/3 tbsp Korean chilli powder
5ml/1 tsp Thai fish sauce
2 garlic cloves, crushed
2.5ml/½ tsp grated fresh root ginger
5ml/1 tsp honey
5ml/1 tsp sesame seeds

Per portion Energy 332kcal/1391kJ; Protein 40.2g; Carbohydrate 18.7g, of which sugars 14.9g; Fat 7.9g, of which saturates 2.6g; Cholesterol 106mg; Calcium 136mg; Fibre 5.9g; Sodium 507mg.

Poached pork wrapped in Chinese leaves

Meltingly tender pork, imbued with the flavours of *doenjang* soybean paste and garlic, is combined with a refreshingly zesty radish stuffing and wrapped in parcels of Chinese leaves. The contrast between the delicate texture of the pork and the crunchy tanginess of the vegetables makes it truly enjoyable. This dish, called *bossam*, is perfect as an appetizer or as a nibble with drinks. **Serves 3–4**

1 Soak the whole head of Chinese leaves in salty water (using 50g/2oz/¼ cup of salt) for about 1 hour, or until the leaves have softened.

2 To make the stuffing, put the white radish into a colander and sprinkle with salt. Leave to stand for 10 minutes, then rinse and transfer to a large bowl. Add the chestnuts, pear and chopped *minari*, watercress or rocket to the bowl and mix together well. Add all the other stuffing ingredients to the bowl, with salt to taste, and stir to coat the vegetable mixture thoroughly.

3 Prepare the poaching liquid by putting the garlic, onion and leek in a large pan. Mix in the *doenjang* soybean paste and sake or rice wine, and then add the pork. Add enough water to cover the pork and bring the liquid to the boil.

4 Cook the pork for 30–40 minutes, until tender. To test if the meat is ready, push a chopstick into the meat – it should pass through cleanly.

5 Drain the Chinese leaves and tear off the leaves, keeping them whole, and place on a serving plate.

6 Transfer the stuffing mixture to a serving dish. Once the pork is cooked, remove it from the liquid and slice it into thin bitesize pieces. Serve with the stuffing and Chinese leaves.

7 To eat, take a slice of the pork and place it on a Chinese leaf. Then spoon a little of the stuffing on to the meat, and wrap it into a parcel before eating it.

Shrimp dip A tasty variation is to dip the pork into a fermented shrimp paste (available at Asian stores) before wrapping it in the leaves.

Doenjang soybean paste gives a lovely roast-chestnut flavour to the pork in this recipe, marrying well with the griddled taste of the meat. The marinade has a mild flavour and gives the pork a succulent barbecue taste. **Serves 3**

  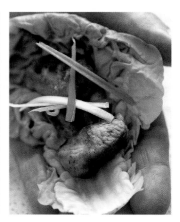

Griddled doenjang pork

675g/1½lb pork loin
2 round (butterhead) lettuces
4 spring onions (scallions), shredded

For the marinade
30ml/2 tbsp *doenjang*, soybean paste
15ml/1 tbsp Thai fish sauce
22.5ml/4½ tsp sugar
1 spring onion (scallion), finely chopped
5ml/1 tsp grated ginger
1 onion, finely chopped
5ml/1 tsp cornflour (cornstarch)
1 garlic clove, crushed
15ml/1 tbsp mirin or rice wine
15ml/1 tbsp milk
ground black pepper

1 Cut the pork into in bitesize pieces.

2 To make the marinade, combine the *doenjang* paste, Thai fish sauce, sugar, spring onion and ginger in a large bowl. Add the onion, cornflour and garlic, and pour in the mirin or rice wine and milk. Season with salt and pepper. Mix well, add the pork and coat with the marinade and leave for 30 minutes.

3 Remove the outer leaves from the heads of lettuce, keeping them whole. Rinse well and place in a serving dish.

4 Place a heavy griddle pan over high heat and once hot reduce to medium heat (the griddle can be used over charcoal). Add the marinated pork and cook well, turning as required. The meat should be well done, with the exterior seared and slightly blackened. Serve by wrapping the meat in a lettuce leaf with pieces of shredded spring onions.

Per portion Energy 355kcal/1493kJ; Protein 50g; Carbohydrate 17.4g, of which sugars 12.4g; Fat 9.9g, of which saturates 3.4g; Cholesterol 142mg; Calcium 74mg; Fibre 1.7g; Sodium 168mg.

This hearty pork and *kimchi* dish is a rich, spicy stew bubbling with flavour and piquancy, traditionally cooked in a heavy clay bowl called a *tukbaege*. The slow cooking allows the flavours to mingle and create complex, enticing taste combinations. **Serves 4**

Kimchi chige

4 dried shiitake mushrooms, soaked in warm water for about 30 minutes
150g/5oz firm tofu
200g/7oz boneless pork chop
300g/11oz cabbage *kimchi* (see page 143)
45ml/3 tbsp vegetable oil
1 garlic clove, crushed
15ml/1 tbsp Korean chilli powder
750ml/1¼ pints/3 cups vegetable stock or water
2 spring onions (scallions), finely sliced
salt

1 When the soaked shiitake mushrooms have reconstituted and become soft, drain and slice them, discarding the stems. Dice the tofu into cubes approximately 2cm/¾in square. Dice the pork into bitesize cubes, and slice the *kimchi* into similar size pieces. Squeeze any excess liquid out of the *kimchi*.

2 Pour the vegetable oil into a pan or wok and place over medium heat. Add the pork and garlic, and sauté until crisp. Once the pork has turned dark brown add the *kimchi* and chilli powder, and stir-fry for 60 seconds more.

3 Add the stock or water and bring to the boil. Add the tofu, mushrooms and spring onions, cover and simmer for 10–15 minutes. Season with salt and serve bubbling from the pan.

Tuna kimchi Create a lighter dish by substituting canned tuna for the pork. Use fish stock to emphasize the flavour.

Soft and firm tofu This recipe is better suited to firm tofu, rather than soft tofu, as it is less likely to break up during cooking.

Per portion Energy 185kcal/770kJ; Protein 15.1g; Carbohydrate 4.2g, of which sugars 4g; Fat 12.1g, of which saturates 1.9g; Cholesterol 32mg; Calcium 234mg; Fibre 1.8g; Sodium 534mg.

Pork belly with sesame dip

675g/1½lb pork belly
2 round (butterhead) lettuces

For the dip
45ml/3 tbsp sesame oil
10ml/2 tsp salt
ground black pepper

For the sauce
45ml/3 tbsp *gochujang* chilli
    paste
75ml/5 tbsp *doenjang* soybean
    paste
2 garlic cloves, crushed
1 spring onion (scallion), finely
    chopped
5ml/1 tsp sesame oil

Samgyupsal is a phenomenally popular pork dish in Korea, and a firm favourite when out socializing, enjoyed with a glass of *soju*. Thinly sliced pork belly is griddled until the outside is crisp, leaving a smooth texture at the centre. The meat is then immersed in a salty sesame dip, before being wrapped in lettuce leaves with a spoonful of red chilli paste to round off the combination of flavours. **Serves 3**

1 Freeze the pork belly for 30 minutes and then slice it very thinly, to about 3mm/⅛in thick. (You could ask the butcher to do this, or buy the meat pre-sliced at an Asian store.)

2 To make the dip, combine the sesame oil, salt and pepper in a small serving bowl.

3 To make the sauce, blend the chilli paste, *doenjang* soybean paste, garlic, spring onion and sesame oil in a bowl, mixing the oil thoroughly into the paste. Transfer to a serving bowl.

4 Remove the outer leaves from the heads of lettuce, keeping them whole. Rinse well and place in a serving dish.

5 Heat a griddle pan or heavy frying pan over high heat (the griddle can be used over charcoal). Add the pork to the pan and cook until the surface of the pork is crisp and golden brown.

6 Serve the pork with the accompanying dishes of lettuce, sesame dip and chilli sauce. To eat, take a strip of pork and dip it into the sesame dip. Then place the meat in a lettuce leaf and add a small spoonful of the chilli sauce. Wrap the lettuce leaf into a parcel and enjoy!

Lettuce Any soft green leaf lettuce can be used; for example, Little Gem (Bibb) or any kind of crisphead lettuce such as iceberg.

Variation You can add other ingredients to the lettuce parcel, if you like. Popular favourites include shredded spring onion (scallion), sliced *kimchi* (see page 143) or sliced raw garlic.

Per portion Energy 991kcal/4093kJ; Protein 37g; Carbohydrate 1.1g, of which sugars 0.6g; Fat 93.1g, of which saturates 31.4g; Cholesterol 162mg; Calcium 37mg; Fibre 1.2g; Sodium 1475mg.

Spicy pork stir-fry

This simple dish, called *cheyuk bokum*, is quick to prepare and makes thinly sliced pork fabulously spicy. The potent flavour of *gochujang* chilli paste predominates in the seasoning for the pork that will set the tastebuds aflame. Serve with a bowl of rice to help counterbalance the fiery chilli character of the dish. **Serves 2**

1 Freeze the pork shoulder for 30 minutes and then slice it thinly, to about 5mm/¼in thick. Cut the onion and carrot into thin strips, and roughly slice the spring onions lengthways.

2 To make the seasoning, combine the seasoning ingredients in a large bowl, mixing together thoroughly to form a paste. If the mixture is too dry, add a splash of water.

3 Heat a wok or large frying pan, and add the vegetable oil. Once the oil is smoking, add the pork, onion, carrot, spring onions and chillies. Stir-fry, keeping the ingredients moving all the time.

4 Once the pork has lightly browned add the seasoning, and thoroughly coat the meat and vegetables. Stir-fry for 2 minutes more, or until the pork is cooked through. Serve immediately with rice and a bowl of miso soup to help neutralize the spicy flavours of the dish.

Marinating An alternative method of preparation is to marinate the pork in the seasoning for an hour before cooking. This creates a tangier version, although the meat is slightly less crispy after cooking.

Cook's tip
• This dish also works well with chicken. Replace the pork shoulder with 400g/14oz chicken thighs and omit the ginger from the seasoning.

400g/14oz pork shoulder
1 onion
½ carrot
2 spring onions (scallions)
15ml/1 tbsp vegetable oil
½ red chilli, finely sliced
½ green chilli, finely sliced
steamed rice and miso
 soup, to serve

For the seasoning
30ml/2 tbsp dark soy sauce
30ml/2 tbsp *gochujang* chilli
 paste
30ml/2 tbsp mirin or rice wine
15ml/1 tbsp Korean chilli powder
1 garlic clove, finely chopped
1 spring onion (scallion), finely
 chopped
15ml/1 tbsp grated fresh root
 ginger
15ml/1 tbsp sesame oil
30ml/2 tbsp sugar
ground black pepper

Per portion Energy 430kcal/1799kJ; Protein 44.1g; Carbohydrate 21.3g, of which sugars 20.4g; Fat 19.2g, of which saturates 4.3g; Cholesterol 126mg; Calcium 44mg; Fibre 1.2g; Sodium 1216mg.

200g/7oz pork fillet
90g/3½oz/¾ cup potato starch
1 egg, beaten
vegetable oil, for deep-frying

For the marinade
5ml/1 tsp dark soy sauce
7.5ml/1½ tsp mirin or rice wine
15ml/1 tbsp finely grated fresh
   root ginger

For the sauce
1 dried shiitake mushroom,
   soaked in warm water for
   about 30 minutes until
   softened
½ onion
½ green (bell) pepper
¼ carrot
25g/1oz pineapple
15ml/1 tbsp vegetable oil
10ml/2 tsp dark soy sauce
60ml/4 tbsp sugar
30ml/2 tbsp cider vinegar

Per portion Energy 727kcal/3035kJ; Protein
32.8g; Carbohydrate 76.5g, of which sugars
39.4g; Fat 32.8g, of which saturates 5.8g;
Cholesterol 272mg; Calcium 85mg; Fibre
2.7g; Sodium 1048mg.

Sweet-and-sour pork

Although very similar to the classic Chinese dish, this Korean version has a much subtler taste and a more delicate texture. Cubes of tender golden pork with a hint of ginger combine with crunchy sweet peppers in a delightfully sticky sauce. A dash of pineapple adds sweetness with a distinctly sour edge, which is intensified by the rice wine and cider vinegar. This makes a perfect lunch served with a selection of *namul* dishes and a bowl of rice. **Serves 2**

1 Add the potato starch to 250ml/8fl oz/1 cup water and leave for 1 hour, during which time the starch should sink to the bottom.

2 Cut the pork into bitesize cubes and place in a bowl. Add the soy sauce, mirin or rice wine, and grated ginger for the marinade, and mix well. Leave to marinate for 20 minutes.

3 When the soaked shiitake mushroom for the sauce has reconstituted and become soft, drain and finely slice it, discarding the stem.

4 Cut the onion, pepper and carrot into bitesize cubes. Finely chop, or grate, the pineapple into a bowl and set aside.

5 Drain the excess water from the top of the starch and water mixture. In a bowl combine the soaked starch with the beaten egg. Add the cubes of pork and evenly coat them in the batter.

6 Fill a wok or medium heavy pan one-third full of vegetable oil and heat over high heat to 170°C/340°F, or when a small piece of bread dropped into the oil browns in 15 seconds. Add the battered pork and deep-fry for 1–2 minutes, or until golden brown. Remove the pork and drain on kitchen paper to remove any excess oil.

7 Next, finish the sauce. Coat a pan with the vegetable oil and place over high heat. Add the onion, pepper and carrot, and stir-fry to soften the vegetables. Add 250ml/8fl oz/1 cup hot water, the soy sauce, sugar and vinegar, and simmer briefly before adding the mushroom and pineapple. Simmer for 1–2 minutes, then add the egg mixture and stir until thickened.

8 Place the fried pork on a serving plate, and pour the sauce liberally over the top. Serve the dish immediately.

Flame-grilling, stews and marinades

 From chilled tartare to fiery *bulgogi,* the Koreans have discovered myriad ways of preparing this hugely popular ingredient. The legacy of the barbecue handed down from the Mongolians remains the most common method of cooking, and the smoky tastes of charcoal and flame-grilling are at the heart of many dishes. While the Chinese prefer pork and the Japanese favour fish, for Koreans there really is no substitute for the richness of flavour and texture that beef offers, with one of the most succulent cuts – beef short ribs – remaining the firm national favourite.

In the traditional dish of *galbi tang* braised short ribs are steeped in a fragrant broth, then slow-cooked with mushrooms and sweet red dates for a wonderfully intense flavour. No New Year's celebration is complete without a bowl of this sumptuous and fragrant stew, a timeless feast-day dish.

Other classic beef dishes rely on sophisticated marinades that have been developed to enhance the taste and texture of the meat. Pear juice is used to bring sweetness to recipes, with a natural fruit acidity that helps to tenderize the meat. Rice wine adds a deep note to the flavour of any marinade, with sesame and ginger also popular to complement the concentrated smoky taste of grilled beef. In contrast to Chinese beef dishes, where the meat is dipped in spices after being roasted or boiled, Korean dishes are seasoned beforehand to allow the complex tastes to imbue the meat before it is grilled and yield a rich, smoky flavour.

In the summer the refreshing succulence of chilled ribbon beef tartare makes it hugely popular, with sesame oil adding richness to the silken texture of the dish. Winter calls for spicier dishes to ward off the cold, and there is none better than the hot and spicy soup *yukgejang* (see page 61). Flavoured with strips of sesame-infused beef this hearty soup has a wonderful red colour imparted by chilli powder, while leeks provide a rich, autumnal warmth.

When it comes to beef recipes there really is no dish to rival *bulgogi* – one of Korea's most famous dishes, and one of its most popular. This recipe grew out of the ancient Korean dish of *maekjuk,* skewered beef roasted over an open fire, and features thin strips of sirloin marinated in sesame, soy sauce and garlic before being grilled to a crisp perfection. As the meat cooks the marinade forms a mouth-watering glaze, which is then traditionally eaten with a spicy dipping sauce.

In the past, beef was reserved for special occasions, with tiny amounts added to dishes to give the impression of that highly prized flavour. However, beef is ubiquitous in the cuisine of modern Korea, with grilled or *gui* dishes being among the nation's most popular.

Fine strips of braised beef are enhanced by a rich, dark soy and garlic sauce, with a piquant kick of root ginger. Muscovado sugar adds an almost imperceptible sweetness, complemented by hot jalapeño chillies. This dish makes an excellent side serving to accompany a larger stew or noodle dish. **Serves 2–3**

Braised beef strips with soy & ginger

450g/1lb beef flank
25g/1oz piece fresh root ginger, peeled
100ml/3½fl oz/scant ½ cup dark soy sauce

75g/3oz light muscovado (brown) sugar
12 garlic cloves, peeled
6 jalapeño chillies

1 Bring a large pan of water to the boil and add the beef. Cook for around 40 minutes until tender. Drain the meat and rinse it in warm water. Leave the beef to cool, then roughly slice it into strips about 5cm/2in long.

2 Place the peeled root ginger in a large pan with the beef and add 300ml/½ pint/1¼ cups water. Bring to the boil, cover and then reduce the heat and simmer for 30 minutes. Skim the fat from the surface of the liquid as the meat cooks. The liquid should have reduced to half its initial volume. Add the soy sauce, muscovado sugar and garlic, and simmer for a further 20 minutes. Then add the jalapeño chillies, and cook for a further 5 minutes.

3 Discard the root ginger, and serve in bowls with generous quantities of the garlic and chillies.

Cook's tip
• If you're using any beef cut other than the flank, the meat should be cut into thin strips or torn by hand to ensure that it is tender when cooked.

Per portion Energy 408kcal/1713kJ; Protein 37.8g; Carbohydrate 34.3g, of which sugars 29.1g; Fat 14.2g, of which saturates 5.7g; Cholesterol 87mg; Calcium 33mg; Fibre 1.4g; Sodium 2472mg.

Instead of a complex marinade, this recipe relies on the taste of high quality sirloin steak. Kneading the meat with salt makes it deliciously tender, and the simple seasoning provides a delicate garlic flavour. Accompanied by a bowl of *doenjang* soup, the smoky aroma and grilled taste of this dish are without equal. **Serves 4**

Kneaded sirloin steak

450g/1lb beef sirloin
2 round (butterhead)
  lettuces

For the marinade
8 garlic cloves, chopped
75g/3oz oyster mushrooms,
  sliced
3 spring onions (scallions),
  finely chopped
20ml/4 tsp mirin or rice
  wine

10ml/2 tsp salt
ground black pepper

**For the spring onion
  mixture**
8 shredded spring onions
  (scallions)
20ml/4 tsp rice vinegar
20ml/4 tsp Korean chilli
  powder
10ml/2 tsp sugar
10ml/2 tsp sesame oil

1 Slice the beef into bitesize strips and place in a bowl. Add the garlic, mushrooms and spring onions. Pour in the mirin or rice wine and add the salt and several twists of black pepper.

2 Mix the marinade together, evenly coating the beef. Knead the meat well to tenderize. Chill, and leave for at least 2 hours.

3 Mix the spring onion ingredients together.

4 Remove the outer leaves from the lettuce and rinse well.

5 Place a griddle pan over medium heat, and add the marinated beef. Cook gently until the meat has darkened, and then remove.

6 Serve by wrapping the meat in a lettuce leaf with a chopstick pinch of the seasoned shredded spring onion mixture.

Per portion Energy 188kcal/786kJ; Protein 27.6g; Carbohydrate 4g, of which sugars 3.9g; Fat 6.9g, of which saturates 2.6g; Cholesterol 57mg; Calcium 26mg; Fibre 0.9g; Sodium 83mg.

Beef & mushroom casserole

150g/5oz beef
2 dried shiitake mushrooms,
   soaked in warm water for
   about 30 minutes until
   softened
25g/1oz enoki mushrooms
1 onion, sliced
400ml/14fl oz/1⅔ cups water
   or beef stock
25g/1oz oyster mushrooms,
   thinly sliced
6 pine mushrooms, cut into
   thin strips
10 spring onions (scallions),
   sliced
2 chrysanthemum leaves, and
   ½ red and ½ green chilli,
   seeded and shredded, to
   garnish
steamed rice, to serve

For the seasoning
30ml/2 tbsp dark soy sauce
3 spring onions (scallions), sliced
2 garlic cloves, crushed
10ml/2 tsp sesame seeds
10ml/2 tsp sesame oil

Per portion Energy 227kcal/945kJ; Protein
21.1g; Carbohydrate 5.5g, of which sugars
4.4g; Fat 13.6g, of which saturates 3.9g;
Cholesterol 44mg; Calcium 72mg; Fibre 2.4g;
Sodium 1125mg.

In this perfect example of a Korean casserole dish, called *beoseot chungol*, wild mushrooms are slow-cooked together in a sauce seasoned with garlic and sesame. Ideal as a warming winter dish, its earthy mushroom flavour is enlivened with spring onions and chillies. **Serves 2**

1 Slice the beef into thin strips and place in a bowl. Add the seasoning ingredients and mix well, coating the beef evenly. Leave to absorb the flavours for 20 minutes.

2 When the soaked shiitake mushrooms have reconstituted and become soft, drain and thinly slice them, discarding the stems. Discard the caps from the enoki mushrooms.

3 Place the seasoned beef and the onion in a heavy pan or flameproof casserole and add the water or beef stock. Add all the mushrooms and the spring onions, and bring to the boil.

4 Once the pan is bubbling reduce the heat and simmer for 20 minutes.

5 Transfer to a serving dish or serve from the casserole. Garnish with the chrysanthemum leaves and shredded chilli, and then serve with steamed rice.

Pine mushrooms Pine mushrooms can be difficult to find; other wild mushrooms will also work well.

For vegetarians Omit the beef for a vegetarian alternative.

Variation Although this recipe should be simmered for a more delicate taste, *chungol* dishes are traditionally served as soon as they have boiled in order to maintain the freshness of the ingredients.

The secret to this dish, called *galbi*, is to marinate the short ribs overnight to allow the flavours to infuse and intensify. The natural fruit acidity in the pear helps to tenderize the meat, and the sake adds a slightly sweet edge. After grilling, the ribs have a refined smoky taste, with a wonderful chewy texture. Short ribs can be bought at most butchers; ask for pieces approximately 5cm/2in square. Stuffed cucumber *kimchi* (see page 144) makes a perfect side dish for *galbi*. **Serves 4**

Barbecued beef short ribs

900g/2lb beef short ribs, cut into 5cm/2in squares
shredded spring onions (scallions), seasoned with Korean chilli powder and rice vinegar, to serve

For the marinade
4 spring onions (scallions), finely sliced
½ onion, finely chopped
1 Asian pear
60ml/4 tbsp dark soy sauce
60ml/4 tbsp sugar
30ml/2 tbsp sesame oil
15ml/1 tbsp sake or rice wine
10ml/2 tsp ground black pepper
5ml/1 tsp sesame seeds
2 garlic cloves, crushed
5ml/1 tsp grated fresh root ginger

1 To make the marinade, place the spring onions and onion in a large bowl. Core and chop the Asian pear, being careful to save the juices, and add to the bowl. Add the remaining marinade ingredients and mix together thoroughly.

2 Add the short ribs to the bowl of marinade, stirring to coat them thickly. Leave to stand for at least 2 hours and preferably overnight, to allow the flavours to permeate and the meat to soften.

3 Heat a heavy griddle pan or frying pan and add the ribs. Keep turning them to cook the meat evenly. When they become crisp and dark brown, serve immediately with a bowl of seasoned shredded spring onions.

Per portion Energy 373kcal/1563kJ; Protein 49.5g; Carbohydrate 9.4g, of which sugars 9.3g; Fat 15.5g, of which saturates 6.7g; Cholesterol 126mg; Calcium 35mg; Fibre 0.5g; Sodium 852mg.

This slow-cooked dish, called *galbitang*, contains short ribs and cubes of Asian radish in an exquisitely rich soup, with fine *dangmyun* noodles just below the surface. A piquant chilli seasoning is added just before serving. **Serves 4**

Simmered short ribs in noodle soup

900g/2lb beef short
  ribs, cut into
  5cm/2in squares
350g/12oz Chinese white
  radish, peeled
5ml/1 tsp salt
90g/3½oz *dangmyun*
  noodles

For the seasoning
45ml/3 tbsp soy sauce
15ml/1 tbsp chilli powder
50g/2oz spring onions
  (scallions), roughly chopped
5ml/1 tsp sesame oil
1 chilli, finely sliced
ground black pepper

1 Soak the ribs in a bowl of cold water for 10 hours to drain the blood, changing the water halfway through once it has discoloured. Drain the ribs. Place the ribs in a large pan, cover with water and place over high heat. Once the water has boiled remove the ribs, rinse them in cold water and set aside.

2 Cut the radish into 2cm/¾in cubes. Place the seasoning ingredients in a bowl and mix thoroughly.

3 Place the ribs in a large heavy pan and cover with 1 litre/ 1¾ pints/4 cups water. Cook over high heat for 20 minutes and add the radish and salt. Reduce the heat and cook for 7 minutes, then add the noodles and cook for 3 minutes more.

4 Ladle the soup into bowls and add a generous spoonful of the seasoning just before serving.

***Dangmyun* noodles** Made from sweet potatoes, *dangmyun* noodles are readily available at Asian stores.

Per portion Energy 437kcal/1830kJ; Protein 52.1g; Carbohydrate 19.8g, of which sugars 3.1g; Fat 17g, of which saturates 6.7g; Cholesterol 126mg; Calcium 40mg; Fibre 1.6g; Sodium 1174mg.

Braised short ribs stew

900g/2lb short ribs, cut into
  5cm/2in squares
3 dried shiitake mushrooms,
  soaked in warm water for
  about 30 minutes until
  softened
½ onion, roughly cubed
½ carrot, roughly cubed
½ potato, roughly cubed
75g/3oz Chinese white radish,
  peeled and roughly diced
2 spring onions (scallions),
  finely sliced
4 chestnuts
2 red dates
30ml/2 tbsp mirin or rice wine
4 gingko nuts, to garnish

For the seasoning
½ Asian pear or kiwi fruit
60ml/4 tbsp light soy sauce
20ml/4 tsp sugar
2 garlic cloves, crushed
5ml/1 tsp finely grated fresh
  root ginger
15ml/1 tbsp sesame seeds
20ml/4 tsp sesame oil
ground black pepper

Koreans are justly proud of their method of cooking spare ribs, which produces a wonderfully intense flavour. The slow cooking blends the earthy tastes of the shiitake mushrooms with the smoky quality of the beef, and the red dates provide a lingering bittersweet tang. This richly coloured stew is a popular feast dish, which is traditionally eaten on New Year's Day. *Namul* vegetables make an ideal accompaniment for this dish, with a dish of radish *kimchi* (see page 145) and a bowl of steamed rice. **Serves 4**

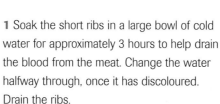

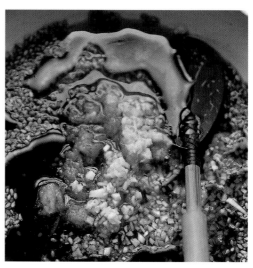

1 Soak the short ribs in a large bowl of cold water for approximately 3 hours to help drain the blood from the meat. Change the water halfway through, once it has discoloured. Drain the ribs.

2 Place the ribs in a large pan, cover with water and put over high heat. Bring to the boil and then remove the ribs and rinse them in cold water. Strain the cooking liquid into a jug (pitcher), and set aside.

3 When the soaked shiitake mushrooms have reconstituted and become soft, drain and slice them, discarding the stems.

4 To make the seasoning, peel and core the Asian pear or kiwi fruit, and grate into a large bowl to catch the juice. Add all the remaining seasoning ingredients and mix them together thoroughly.

5 Use a knife to make deep cuts in the ribs and place them in the bowl of seasoning. Coat the meat, working the mixture well into the slits, and leave it to absorb the flavours for 20 minutes.

6 Transfer the ribs and seasoning mixture to a large, heavy pan. Add the sliced mushrooms, chunks of onion, carrot, potato, radish and spring onions. Then add the whole chestnuts and red dates. Pour 200ml/7floz/ scant 1 cup water over the ingredients and set the pan over high heat.

7 Once the liquid begins to boil add the mirin or rice wine and cover the pan. Reduce the heat and simmer for 1 hour, or until the meat has become very tender. If necessary, top up the level of liquid from the jug so that there is enough liquid to cover all of the ingredients.

8 Serve with a garnish of gingko nuts.

Per portion Energy 533kcal/2223kJ; Protein 49.6g; Carbohydrate 16.7g, of which sugars 10.3g; Fat 30.1g, of which saturates 9g; Cholesterol 126mg; Calcium 35mg; Fibre 1.5g; Sodium 147mg.

Bulgogi is one of Korea's most popular dishes. Thin strips of sirloin are marinated in sesame oil and soy sauce, then grilled over a charcoal brazier. The meat with its delicious glaze is often enjoyed with a piquant dipping sauce or fresh green leaves. **Serves 4**

Griddled beef with sesame & soy

800g/1¾lb sirloin steak

For the marinade
4 spring onions (scallions)
½ onion
1 Asian pear
60ml/4 tbsp dark soy sauce

60ml/4 tbsp sugar
30ml/2 tbsp sesame oil
10ml/2 tsp ground black pepper
5ml/1 tsp sesame seeds
2 garlic cloves, crushed
15ml/1 tbsp lemonade

1 Finely slice the steak, and lightly tenderize by bashing with a meat mallet or rolling pin before cutting into bitesize strips.

2 Roughly shred one of the spring onions and set aside for a garnish. Finely slice the remaining spring onions, the onion and pear. Combine the marinade ingredients in a large bowl to form a paste, adding a little water if necessary.

3 Mix the beef in with the marinade, making sure that it is well coated. Leave in the refrigerator for at least 30 minutes or up to 2 hours (if left longer the meat will become too salty).

4 Heat a griddle pan gently. Add the meat and cook over medium heat. The marinade will form a glaze over the meat, and the juices can be collected after cooking and eaten with rice. Once the meat has darkened and is cooked through, transfer it to a large serving dish, garnish with the spring onion and serve.

Serving *Bulgogi* is delicious wrapped in lettuce leaves, or dipped in a blend of soy sauce, crushed garlic and a drop of lemon juice. Serve with rice, *kimchi* and *namul* vegetables.

Per portion Energy 330kcal/1382kJ; Protein 47.3g; Carbohydrate 8.2g, of which sugars 8.1g; Fat 12.1g, of which saturates 4.5g; Cholesterol 102mg; Calcium 22mg; Fibre 0.2g; Sodium 141mg.

Succulent raw beef is here perfectly harmonized with sweet Asian pear, garlic and egg yolk. The fresh beef is cut into fine ribbons and tossed in a sesame oil seasoning. Its delicate, silky texture is contrasted with toasted pine nuts and lettuce. Use the freshest cuts of meat for this recipe to ensure the best flavour. **Serves 4**

Ribbon beef tartare

400g/14oz beef, skirt (flank)
  or topside loin
1 Asian pear
1 lettuce
30ml/2 tbsp pine nuts
1 egg yolk
3 garlic cloves, thinly sliced

For the seasoning
60ml/4 tbsp soy sauce
30ml/2 tbsp sugar
1 spring onion (scallion),
  finely chopped
1 garlic clove, crushed
15ml/1 tbsp sesame seeds
20ml/4 tsp sesame oil
ground black pepper

1 Freeze the beef for 30 minutes before preparation.

2 Cut the Asian pear into thin julienne strips. Line a serving platter with lettuce leaves and arrange the pear around the outside, leaving a space in the centre.

3 Toast the pine nuts in a dry pan until lightly browned. Set aside.

4 Remove the beef from the freezer and slice into ribbon-thin strips, discarding any fatty sections. Put the beef into a bowl, and add all the seasoning ingredients. Mix thoroughly by hand, kneading the meat gently.

5 Place the seasoned beef into the middle of the lettuce-lined platter, and gently lay the unbroken egg yolk on the top. Sprinkle with the pine nuts and sliced garlic, and serve. To eat, break the egg yolk and mix it with the beef. Transfer to individual bowls or plates. Diners should eat the beef with a little pear and garlic for the best possible combination of flavours.

Per portion Energy 263kcal/1106kJ; Protein 25.8g; Carbohydrate 14.9g, of which sugars 14.2g; Fat 11.6g, of which saturates 2.6g; Cholesterol 100mg; Calcium 70mg; Fibre 2.2g; Sodium 797mg.

Beef with glass noodles

250g/9oz *dangmyun* or glass
  noodles
5 dried shiitake mushrooms,
  soaked in warm water for
  about 30 minutes until
  softened
275g/10oz beef
1 carrot
90g/3½oz spinach
15ml/1 tbsp sesame oil, plus
  extra for drizzling
2 eggs, beaten
25ml/1½ tbsp vegetable oil
1 spring onion (scallion),
  roughly sliced
salt
sesame seeds, to garnish

For the marinade
2 garlic cloves, crushed
30ml/2 tbsp soy sauce
15ml/1 tbsp sesame oil
5ml/1 tsp sugar
10ml/2 tsp mirin or rice wine

For the seasoning
30ml/2 tbsp soy sauce
15ml/1 tbsp sugar
1 garlic clove, crushed

One of Korea's most popular noodle dishes, *chapchae* is traditionally served at celebrations. Quick and easy to cook, the delicate texture of the glass noodles combines perfectly with the crunchy vegetables and rich, sesame-infused strips of beef. **Serves 4**

1 Soak the *dangmyun* noodles in warm water for 30 minutes. When the soaked shiitake mushrooms have reconstituted and become soft, drain and slice them, discarding the stems.

2 Combine all the marinade ingredients in a large bowl. Slice the beef into thin strips and add it, with the mushrooms, to the bowl of marinade. Coat well and leave to marinate for 20 minutes.

3 Meanwhile, cut the carrot into thin julienne strips. Bring a pan of water to the boil. Blanch the spinach for 1 minute then rinse it under cold running water. Squeeze out any excess liquid and season with salt and 15ml/1 tbsp sesame oil.

4 Season the beaten eggs with a pinch of salt. Coat a frying pan with 10ml/2 tsp vegetable oil and heat over medium heat. Add the beaten egg and make a thin omelette, browning gently on each side. Remove from the pan and cut into thin strips, then set aside.

5 Coat a large frying pan or wok with the remaining vegetable oil and heat over medium heat. Add the marinated beef and mushrooms, then stir-fry until the meat is golden brown. Remove the beef and mushrooms, and set them aside.

6 Use the same pan (preserving any cooking juices from the meat) to stir-fry the carrot, spinach and spring onion. Add the seasoning ingredients to the vegetables in the pan and coat well. Reduce the heat under the pan. Stir in the beef and mushrooms, mixing all the ingredients well.

7 Drizzle with a little sesame oil and transfer to a shallow serving dish. Garnish the mixture with the strips of omelette and a sprinkling of sesame seeds before serving.

Cellophane noodles *Dangmyun* noodles are best for this dish, although glass noodles (also known as cellophane or bean thread noodles) will work almost as well.

Per portion Energy 458kcal/1911kJ; Protein 22.8g; Carbohydrate 54.5g, of which sugars 3.4g; Fat 15.8g, of which saturates 4.2g; Cholesterol 135mg; Calcium 71mg; Fibre 1g; Sodium 390mg.

Beef & vegetable rice

400g/14oz/2 cups short grain
rice or pudding rice, rinsed
a drop of sunflower oil
1 sheet dried seaweed
4 quail's eggs
vegetable oil, for shallow-frying
sesame seeds, to garnish

For the marinated beef
30ml/2 tbsp dark soy sauce
15ml/1 tbsp garlic, crushed
15ml/1 tbsp sliced spring onions
    (scallions)
5ml/1 tsp sesame oil
5ml/1 tsp rice wine
200g/7oz beef, shredded
10ml/2 tsp vegetable oil
salt and ground black pepper

For the *namul* vegetables
150g/5oz white radish, peeled
1 courgette (zucchini)
2 carrots
150g/5oz/generous ½ cup soya
    beansprouts, trimmed
150g/5oz fern fronds (optional)
6 dried shiitake mushrooms,
    soaked in warm water for about
    30 minutes until softened
½ cucumber

For the *namul* seasoning
5ml/1 tsp sugar
12.5ml/2½ tsp salt
30ml/2 tbsp sesame oil
5ml/1 tsp crushed garlic
a splash of dark soy sauce
1.5ml/¼ tsp chilli powder
5ml/1 tsp sesame seeds
vegetable oil, for stir-frying

For the *gochujang* sauce
15ml/1 tbsp *gochujang*
7.5ml/1½ tsp sugar or honey
10ml/2 tsp sesame oil

Per portion Energy 645kcal/2688kJ; Protein
23.7g; Carbohydrate 88.5g, of which sugars
7.7g; Fat 21.4g, of which saturates 4.4g;
Cholesterol 86mg; Calcium 73mg; Fibre 2.3g;
Sodium 1781mg.

In this dish, called *bibimbap*, a medley of vegetables garnish a bed of pearly steamed rice, which is then seasoned with sesame and soy sauce. Lightly browned beef is added, and the dish is topped with a fried quail's egg and a scoop of *gochujang* chilli paste. **Serves 4**

1 Place the rice in a pan and add water to 5mm/¼in above the rice. Add the sunflower oil, cover and bring to the boil. Lower the heat and steam. Do not remove the lid. After 12–15 minutes turn off the heat and steam for 5 more minutes.

2 For the marinade, blend the soy sauce, garlic, spring onions, sesame oil, rice wine, and salt and pepper. Add the beef, mix well and marinate for 1 hour. Roll up the seaweed and slice into strips.

3 Thoroughly mix the ingredients for the gochujang sauce and place in a serving bowl.

4 Cut the white radish, courgette and carrots into thin julienne strips.

5 For the radish, blend 5ml/1 tsp sugar, 5ml/1 tsp salt and 5ml/1 tsp sesame oil, with 2.5ml/½ tsp crushed garlic, and flash-fry. Use to coat the radish julienne. Transfer to a plate.

6 Blend 5ml/1 tsp salt and 5ml/1 tsp sesame oil with 2.5ml/½ tsp crushed garlic and a splash of water. Use to coat the courgette julienne. Heat 5ml/1 tsp vegetable oil in a wok and flash-fry the courgette until softened. Transfer to the plate.

7 Briefly cook the soya beansprouts in a pan of boiling water. Combine 15ml/1 tbsp sesame oil with 2.5ml/½ tsp salt, 1.5ml/¼ tsp chilli powder and 2.5ml/½ tsp sesame seeds. Sweeten with a pinch of sugar and use to coat the soya beansprouts. Transfer to the plate.

8 Parboil the fern fronds, if using, and drain. Stir-fry in 5ml/1 tsp sesame oil, with a splash of soy sauce and 2.5ml/½ tsp sesame seeds.

9 Drain and slice the shiitake mushrooms, discarding the stems. Quickly stir-fry in 5ml/1 tsp vegetable oil and season with a pinch of salt. Transfer to the plate.

10 Seed the cucumber, cut into thin julienne strips and transfer to the plate.

11 Heat 10ml/2 tsp vegetable oil in the wok and stir-fry the beef until tender and golden brown.

12 Divide the rice among four bowls and arrange the *namul* vegetables and beef on top. Fry the quail's eggs, and place one in the centre of each bowl. Garnish with a sprinkling of sesame seeds and ribbons of dried seaweed. Serve with the *gochujang* sauce.

Scallops and squid to whelks and prawns

Surrounded on three sides by water, the Korean peninsula is rich in seafood. Warm and cold water currents yield a varied bounty, and the markets offer every species imaginable. Korean cuisine makes the most of this deliciously fresh seafood, with cooking techniques ranging from salads of seafood with spicy dressings to slow-cooked casseroles overflowing with prawns, squid and blue crab.

Korean seafood salads are rich in flavour and texture, and customarily have a delicious contrast, with the chilled seafood offset by the spiciness of the dressing. The spicy whelk salad uses chilli and garlic to add piquancy to the recipe, while the presence of cucumber provides a refreshing quality that completes the dish. The other salad enjoyed in Korea during the summer is a classic medley of chilled seafood with fiery mustard dressing. Simple to prepare and deliciously sharp, this dish is a common choice for a snack or light lunch on a hot afternoon.

As with so many Korean dishes, *gochujang* red chilli paste plays a major role in flavouring seafood. Stir-fried squid is tossed with spring onions (scallions), cucumber and seaweed, and coated in a dressing to create a dish that blends spiciness with the mellow texture of the seafood and the crunchiness of the vegetables.

However, milder ingredients such as rice wine and watercress are also used to complement the more delicate flavours of fish and shellfish. As such a plentiful variety of fresh and saltwater fish is available in Korea there is a wide range of recipes for cooking the various species indigenous to the peninsula. A memorable dish combines braised mackerel with Chinese white radish and sake, the oily fish acting as a perfect companion for the dry, clean taste of the rice wine.

There are a number of delicious seafood stews that adorn the winter table, and feature rich, spicy mixtures of shellfish, vegetables and seasonings. The traditional Korean preparation of octopus relies on a chilli sauce and jalapeño chillies to give it a kick fierce enough to keep the cold at bay, with a little maple syrup to sweeten the delicious charred taste of the dish.

However it is sometimes the simplest dishes that are the most appealing, and allow the natural taste of the seafood to shine through. A wonderful showcase for the fragrant, creamy taste of scallops combines them with enoki mushrooms and strips of egg-yolk omelette – but, as always, it would not be complete without a little chilli. Aromatic and flavoursome, these dishes are a tantalizing fusion of fresh fish, succulent shellfish, vegetables and spices with a quintessentially Korean taste.

Oily fish such as mackerel
is a perfect match for the
clean, dry taste of sake.
Garlic and chilli mute the
strong flavour of the fish,
while the diced radish
absorbs all the flavours
of the cooking liquid for a
unique and delicious taste.
Serves 2–3

Braised mackerel with white radish

1 large mackerel, filleted
300g/11oz Chinese white
   radish, peeled
120ml/4fl oz/½ cup light soy
   sauce
30ml/2 tbsp sake or
   rice wine
30ml/2 tbsp maple syrup

3 garlic cloves, crushed
10ml/2 tsp Korean chilli
   powder
½ onion, chopped
1 red chilli, seeded
   and sliced
1 green chilli, seeded
   and sliced

1 Slice the mackerel into medium-size pieces. Cut the radish
into 2.5cm/1in cubes, and then arrange evenly across the base
of a large pan. Cover with a layer of mackerel.

2 Pour the soy sauce over the fish and add 200ml/7fl oz/ scant
1 cup water, the sake or rice wine, and the maple syrup.
Sprinkle the crushed garlic and chilli powder into the pan, and
gently stir the liquid, trying not to disturb the fish and radish.
Add the onion and sliced chillies, and cover the pan.

3 Place over high heat and bring the liquid to the boil. Reduce
the heat and simmer for 8–10 minutes, or until the fish is
tender, spooning the soy liquid over the fish as it cooks. Ladle
into bowls and serve immediately.

Variation If Chinese white radish is not available then
potatoes make a good alternative. They will give a sweeter,
more delicate flavour to the fish, while a pinch of coriander
(cilantro) leaves will add more of a Thai flavour to the recipe.

Per portion Energy 207kcal/861kJ; Protein 13.4g; Carbohydrate 11.4g, of which
sugars 10.9g; Fat 11g, of which saturates 2.3g; Cholesterol 36mg; Calcium
33mg; Fibre 1.2g; Sodium 81mg.

Here octopus is stir-fried to give it a rich meaty texture, then smothered in a fiery chilli sauce. The dish combines the charred octopus flavour with *gochujang* spiciness and the zing of jalapeño chillies. Serve with steamed rice and a bowl of soup. **Serves 2**

Fiery octopus

2 small octopuses, cleaned and gutted
15ml/1 tbsp vegetable oil
½ onion, sliced 5mm/¼in thick
¼ carrot, thinly sliced
½ leek, thinly sliced
75g/3oz jalapeño chillies, trimmed
2 garlic cloves, crushed

10ml/2 tsp Korean chilli powder
5ml/1 tsp dark soy sauce
45ml/3 tbsp *gochujang* chilli paste
30ml/2 tbsp mirin or rice wine
15ml/1 tbsp maple syrup
sesame oil and sesame seeds, to garnish

1 First blanch the octopuses in boiling water to soften slightly. Drain well, and cut into pieces approximately 5cm/2in long.

2 Heat the oil in a frying pan over medium-high heat and add the onion, carrot, leek and jalapeño chillies. Stir-fry for 3 minutes.

3 Add the octopus and garlic, and sprinkle over the chilli powder. Stir-fry for 3–4 minutes, or until the octopus is tender. Add the soy sauce, *gochujang* paste, mirin or rice wine, and maple syrup. Mix well and stir-fry for 1 minute more.

4 Transfer to a serving platter, and garnish with a drizzle of sesame oil and a sprinkling of sesame seeds.

Tone it down If the taste is too fiery mix some softened vermicelli noodles in with the stir-fry to dilute the chilli paste.

Tenderizing To make the octopus more tender, knead it with a handful of plain (all-purpose) flour and rinse in salted water.

Per portion Energy 235kcal/988kJ; Protein 28.6g; Carbohydrate 13.2g, of which sugars 11.9g; Fat 8g, of which saturates 1.2g; Cholesterol 72mg; Calcium 76mg; Fibre 2.4g; Sodium 204mg.

Seafood salad in mustard dressing

50g/2oz squid
50g/2oz king prawns (jumbo
  shrimp)
50g/2oz jellyfish (optional)
50g/2oz cooked whelks
90g/3½oz Asian pear
⅓ carrot
½ medium cucumber
25g/1oz Chinese leaves
  (Chinese cabbage), shredded
25g/1oz chestnuts, sliced
25g/1oz crab meat or seafood
  stick

For the dressing
15ml/1 tbsp ready-made
  English (hot) mustard
30ml/2 tbsp sugar
15ml/1 tbsp milk
45ml/3 tbsp cider vinegar
5ml/1 tsp chilli oil
2.5ml/½ tsp dark soy sauce
5ml/1 tsp salt

Per portion Energy 206kcal/872kJ; Protein
18g; Carbohydrate 29.8g, of which sugars
23.9g; Fat 2.4g, of which saturates 0.6g;
Cholesterol 230mg; Calcium 62mg; Fibre
2.4g; Sodium 1282mg.

The key ingredient in this dish is English mustard. It gives the dish a pleasant heat, perfectly complementing the seafood flavours with a unique and slightly mysterious taste. Or, for a more authentic taste, use Korean mustard. Simple to prepare, this dish is a perfect quick snack or appetizer. **Serves 2**

1 Wash the squid carefully, rinsing off any ink. Holding the body firmly, pull away the head and tentacles. If the ink sac is intact, remove it and discard. Pull out all the innards including the long transparent "pen". Peel off and discard the thin purple skin on the body, but keep the two small side fins. Slice the head across just under the eyes, severing the tentacles. Discard the rest of the head. Squeeze the tentacles at the head end to push out the round beak in the centre and discard. Rinse the pouch and tentacles well. (Your fishmonger will prepare squid for you.) Score the squid with a crisscross pattern, and slice into strips about 2cm/¾in wide.

2 Hold each prawn between two fingers and pull off the tail shell. Twist off the head. Peel away the soft body shell and the small claws. Make a shallow cut down the centre of the curved back of the prawn. Pull out the black vein with a cocktail stick (toothpick). Rinse well. Slice the prawns and jellyfish into similar sized pieces.

3 Bring a pan of lightly salted water to the boil and blanch the squid, prawns and jellyfish for 3 minutes, then drain. Thinly slice the whelks.

4 Peel the Asian pear. Cut the pear and carrot into thin julienne strips. Seed the cucumber and cut into thin julienne strips.

5 Combine all the dressing ingredients in a bowl until well blended. Take a large serving platter and arrange the julienne vegetables, Chinese leaves and chestnuts in rows, or fan them around the centre of the plate. Add the seafood, including the crab meat or seafood stick. Pour over the dressing and chill in the refrigerator before serving.

Jellyfish Although jellyfish makes an exotic addition to this dish, it can be very difficult to find. Some Asian stores may stock it, but outside the Far East it is a rare delicacy.

Squid & seaweed with chilli dressing

This chilled seafood salad makes a great appetizer, and really stimulates the appetite. The flavours of chilli and rice vinegar are balanced by sweet maple syrup, with the kelp providing a tantalizing aroma and taste. **Serves 2**

1 Wash the squid carefully, rinsing off any ink. Holding the body firmly, pull away the head and tentacles. If the ink sac is intact, remove it and discard. Pull out all the innards including the long transparent "pen". Peel off and discard the thin purple skin on the body, but keep the two small side fins. Slice the head across just under the eyes, severing the tentacles. Discard the rest of the head. Squeeze the tentacles at the head end to push out the round beak in the centre and discard. Rinse the pouch and tentacles well. (Your fishmonger will prepare squid for you.) Use a sharp knife to score the squid with a crisscross pattern, and slice into generous pieces about 4cm/1½in long.

2 Soak the kelp in cold water for 20 minutes and blanch in boiling water for 1 minute, draining it almost immediately to retain its texture and colour. Squeeze any excess water from the leaves by hand. Roughly chop the kelp into bitesize pieces.

3 Put the thinly sliced cucumber in a colander and sprinkle with salt. Leave for 10 minutes, and then pour away any excess liquid.

4 Combine all the dressing ingredients in a large bowl.

5 Bring a pan of water to the boil over high heat. Blanch the squid for 3 minutes, stirring constantly, then drain under cold running water. Place the squid, cucumber and kelp on a serving platter and pour the dressing over the dish. Chill in the refrigerator, and sprinkle with the sesame seeds, spring onions and chillies before serving.

Seaweed Kelp is usually available at Asian stores and health food stores, but if you can't find it try spinach with a squeeze of lemon juice. For real authenticity use fresh kelp collected from clean sea water, but wash it thoroughly in fresh cold water first.

400g/14oz squid
180g/7oz dried kelp, roughly chopped
2 cucumbers, thinly sliced
10ml/2 tsp sesame seeds
6 spring onions (scallions), finely chopped
2 dried red chillies, finely chopped
salt

For the dressing
30ml/2 tbsp rice vinegar
2 garlic cloves, crushed
60ml/4 tbsp *gochujang* chilli paste
60ml/4 tbsp maple syrup
5ml/1 tbsp grated fresh root ginger

Per portion Energy 321kcal/1354kJ; Protein 35.6g; Carbohydrate 30g, of which sugars 27.3g; Fat 7.3g, of which saturates 1.3g; Cholesterol 450mg; Calcium 247mg; Fibre 3.3g; Sodium 433mg.

This salad is a popular appetizer, often eaten as a snack with drinks. The saltiness of the whelks mingles with the heat of the chilli and the refreshing coolness of the cucumber, creating a captivating combination of tastes and textures. **Serves 2**

Spicy whelk salad

300g/11oz cooked whelks, drained
1/2 medium cucumber
1 carrot
2 spring onions (scallions)
1 red chilli, finely sliced
1 green chilli, finely sliced
1/2 onion, finely sliced

For the dressing
45ml/3 tbsp soy sauce
45ml/3 tbsp sugar
45ml/3 tbsp rice vinegar
30ml/2 tbsp Korean chilli powder
10ml/2 tsp garlic, crushed
5ml/1 tsp sesame seeds
2.5ml/1/2 tsp salt
2.5ml/1/2 tsp ground pepper
5ml/1 tsp sesame oil

1 Wash and drain the whelks and slice them into pieces roughly 1cm/1/2in long.

2 Seed the cucumber and then slice it into long, thin matchstick strips. Cut the carrot into thin julienne strips and slice the spring onions into thin strips.

3 Blend all the dressing ingredients in a bowl, mixing them together thoroughly.

4 Combine the whelks with the cucumber, carrot, chillies, onion and spring onions in a large salad bowl. Pour over the dressing and toss the salad before serving.

Per portion Energy 215kcal/907kJ; Protein 25g; Carbohydrate 17g, of which sugars 14.1g; Fat 5.7g, of which saturates 1.1g; Cholesterol 338mg; Calcium 69mg; Fibre 1.8g; Sodium 1737mg.

Fragrant steamed scallops are here given a spicy twist with shreds of chilli pepper. Delicate enoki mushrooms and strips of sautéed egg yolk match the elegant flavours of the seafood, and shredded seaweed and lemon zest are an attractive garnish. **Serves 2**

Spicy scallops with enoki mushrooms

5 scallops, with shells
30ml/2 tbsp vegetable oil
10ml/2 tsp sesame oil
2 egg yolks, beaten
1 sheet dried seaweed
1 red chilli, seeded and finely sliced

$^1/_2$ green (bell) pepper, finely sliced
65g/2$^1/_2$oz enoki mushrooms
salt and ground white pepper
grated rind of 1 lemon

1 Scrub the scallop shells. Cut the hinge muscles at the scallop's base. Lift off the rounded shell. Scrape away the beard-like fringe next to the white scallop with its orange coral, and remove the intestinal thread. Ease the scallop and coral away from the shell.

2 Heat 15ml/1 tbsp vegetable oil in a wok and stir-fry the scallops until browned. Season with sesame oil, salt and pepper.

3 Place the scallop shells into a pan of boiling water and drain. Add 10ml/2 tsp oil to the wok and heat over a low flame. Pour in the beaten egg yolks and add a pinch of salt. Cook to form a thin omelette. Once set, remove from the pan and slice into strips.

4 Cut the seaweed into julienne strips. Add the chilli and pepper to the pan, adding oil if required, and stir-fry with a pinch of salt.

5 Place the scallop shells in a steamer, and set one scallop on each shell. Place the pepper mixture, some omelette strips and some mushrooms on each shell, and steam for 4 minutes.

6 Garnish with the seaweed strips and a sprinkle of lemon rind.

Per portion Energy 325kcal/1356kJ; Protein 27.2g; Carbohydrate 6.8g, of which sugars 3.1g; Fat 21.3g, of which saturates 3.8g; Cholesterol 249mg; Calcium 59mg; Fibre 1.2g; Sodium 193mg.

King prawns with pine nut dressing

6 large king prawns (jumbo
    shrimp)
20g/³⁄₄oz fresh root ginger,
    peeled and sliced
15ml/1 tbsp mirin or rice wine
¹⁄₂ cucumber
75g/3oz bamboo shoots, sliced
90g/3¹⁄₂oz beef flank
15ml/1 tbsp vegetable oil
salt and ground white pepper

For the dressing
60ml/4 tbsp pine nuts
10ml/2 tsp sesame oil
2.5ml/¹⁄₂ tsp salt
ground black pepper

Per portion Energy 416kcal/1724kJ; Protein
24.7g; Carbohydrate 3.5g, of which sugars
2.7g; Fat 33.8g, of which saturates 4.3g;
Cholesterol 124mg; Calcium 62mg; Fibre
1.5g; Sodium 619mg.

This seafood dish is a sophisticated appetizer passed down from the royal banqueting tables of a bygone age. Succulent steamed prawns are mixed with shredded beef and crunchy bamboo shoots then coated with a rich pine nut dressing to create a scintillating chilled dish. **Serves 2**

1 Hold each prawn between two fingers and gently pull off the tail shell. Remove the small claws beneath the body. Rinse well. Prepare a steamer over a pan of boiling water, with a bowl in place under the steamer to catch any liquid. Place the prawns in the steamer with the ginger, and pour over the mirin or rice wine. Season with salt and pepper. Steam for 8 minutes.

2 Seed the cucumber and slice it lengthways into thin strips. Place in a colander and sprinkle with salt, then leave to stand for 5 minutes. Squeeze gently to remove any excess liquid.

3 Remove the prawns from the steamer, discarding the ginger. Remove the bowl of liquid from beneath the steamer and set it aside.

4 Blanch the bamboo shoots in boiling water for 30 seconds. Remove, slice and sprinkle with salt. Add the beef to the boiling water and cook until tender. Drain and leave to cool.

5 Remove the heads and shells from the prawns. Make a shallow cut down the centre of the curved back of each prawn. Pull out the black vein with a cocktail stick (toothpick) or your fingers, and then rinse the prawn thoroughly. Slice them into 2cm/³⁄₄in pieces. Transfer to the refrigerator.

6 Slice the beef thinly, cut into bitesize pieces and chill in the refrigerator. Coat a frying pan or wok with the vegetable oil and quickly stir-fry the cucumber and bamboo shoots until they have softened. Cool then chill in the refrigerator.

7 To make the dressing, roughly grind the pine nuts in a mortar and pestle and then transfer to a bowl. Add 45ml/3 tbsp of the prawn liquid from the bowl and add the sesame oil with a pinch of salt and pepper. Mix well.

8 Set all the chilled ingredients on a platter and pour over the dressing before serving.

Blending fresh and preserved flavours

On the high mountain slopes of Korea a thriving array of wild vegetables are found. Throughout history this abundant variety of vegetables has provided a rich source of nourishment and of inspiration for the national cuisine.

Vegetables are transformed using a variety of preparation and cooking techniques, and their flavours are blended in unique and exotic ways. A simple medley of wild mushrooms provides delicious earthy flavours, whereas an extravagant fusion of seasoned vegetables, beef and rice makes a satisfying centrepiece to any meal.

Koreans enjoy combining textures and tastes in their cooking, and sophisticated sauces often provide exciting combinations of flavour. A classic example uses stuffed aubergines (eggplants) which are then smothered in a rich rice wine and ginger sauce, with subtle notes of garlic, seaweed and dark soy sauce providing an indefinable taste just beneath the surface. These wonderfully complex combinations of flavours are integral to seasoning vegetable dishes in Korea, and add a superb depth to even the most basic of recipes. A simple salad of bamboo, for instance, is brought to life by a delicious combination of sweet and savoury in the form of a persimmon and dark soy dressing.

Vegetable stews are an essential part of many Korean meals, and unlike the light soups have real filling, hearty quality. Served in a heavy stone pot, and brought still bubbling to the table, a classic stew will have a base of *doenjang* soybean paste and a medley of root vegetables and piquant spices imparting a delectable warmth, ideal for any cold winter evening.

Another common ingredient in Korean cooking is tofu, and many dishes use the versatile soybean curd as a base, offsetting the creamy texture and mild flavour with potent spices. These dishes are packed full of healthy ingredients and captivating flavours, and their unique appearance is sure to tempt any appetite.

Tofu dishes are cooked in a range of ways, with pan-frying, stewing and blanching all creating a different texture and flavour. Pan-fried tofu provides a wonderful contrast between the crispy flavoursome coating and the smooth, creamy centre of the bean-curd, and other ingredients are often blended with the dish, traditionally a zesty stuffing of chestnuts and green chillies.

Blanched tofu has a milder flavour, and will be more inclined to take on the qualities of other ingredients in the dish. A classic dressing for blanched beancurd is made from dark soy sauce and spring onion (scallion), with the tofu absorbing the heavy smoky tastes to create a mouth-watering dish with a velvety texture.

One of the distinguishing aspects of Korean cooking is the ability to blend the flavours of fresh and preserved ingredients, and a perfect example of this is the dish of tofu and stir-fried *kimchi*. The light nutty freshness of the beancurd is complemented by the rich fermented spicy quality of the *kimchi*, creating a sensation that unifies the distinctive tastes of both ingredients.

2 aubergines (eggplants)
1 egg
25ml/1½ tbsp vegetable oil
90g/3½oz/scant ½ cup minced
  (ground) beef
15ml/1 tbsp mirin or rice wine
15ml/1 tbsp dark soy sauce
1 garlic clove, crushed
5ml/1 tsp sesame oil
1 red chilli, seeded and
  shredded
1 green chilli, seeded and
  shredded
salt and ground black pepper
steamed rice, to serve

For the sauce
30ml/2 tbsp mirin or rice wine
30ml/2 tbsp dark soy sauce
5ml/1 tsp fresh root ginger,
  peeled and grated
1 sheet dried seaweed

Stuffed aubergine with rice wine & ginger sauce

The succulent beef filling complements the creamy texture of the braised aubergine beautifully, and the whole dish is infused by the flavours of rice wine and ginger, with a fiery kick supplied by chillies. **Serves 2**

1 Clean the aubergines, and cut into slices about 2.5cm/1in thick. Make two cross slits down the length of each slice, making sure not to cut all the way through. Sprinkle with a little salt and set aside.

2 Beat the egg and season with a pinch of salt. Coat a frying pan with 10ml/2 tsp vegetable oil and heat over medium heat. Add the beaten egg and make a thin omelette, browning gently on each side. Remove from the pan and cut into thin strips. Cool then chill in the refrigerator.

3 Heat the remaining vegetable oil in a frying pan over high heat. Cut the seaweed into strips and stir fry with the minced beef, mirin or rice wine, soy sauce and garlic. Once the beef is cooked, drizzle with the sesame oil and set aside.

4 Place the chillies in a bowl. Add the egg strips and the beef, and mix together well. Rinse the salt from the aubergines and stuff each slice with a little of the beef mixture.

5 Place all the ingredients for the sauce into a frying pan, add 200ml/7fl oz/scant 1 cup of water and salt to taste, and heat over medium heat. Once the sauce is blended and bubbling add the stuffed aubergine slices. Spoon the sauce over the aubergines and simmer for 15 minutes, or until the aubergines are soft and the skin has become shiny.

6 Transfer to a shallow dish and serve with steamed rice.

Bamboo shoot salad with persimmon & soy dressing

Crunchy bamboo combines perfectly with seasoned beef, with persimmon adding an appetizing sweetness. Peppery watercress and crisp beansprouts make this into a refreshing salad, lightly seasoned with a sweet–sour soy dressing. **Serves 1–2**

200g/7oz bamboo shoots
2 dried shiitake mushrooms, soaked in warm water for about 30 minutes until softened
50g/2oz beef flank, thinly sliced
25ml/1$\frac{1}{2}$ tbsp vegetable oil
90g/3$\frac{1}{2}$oz/scant $\frac{1}{2}$ cup beansprouts
1 egg
90g/3$\frac{1}{2}$oz watercress or rocket (arugula)
salt
$\frac{1}{2}$ red chilli, seeded and thinly sliced, to garnish

For the seasoning
7.5ml/1$\frac{1}{2}$ tsp dark soy sauce
10g/$\frac{1}{4}$oz red persimmon, finely chopped
$\frac{1}{2}$ spring onion (scallion), finely chopped
1 garlic clove, crushed
5ml/1 tsp sesame seeds
2.5ml/$\frac{1}{2}$ tsp sesame oil
ground white pepper

For the dressing
60ml/4 tbsp dark soy sauce
60ml/4 tbsp water
30ml/2 tbsp rice vinegar
40g/1$\frac{1}{2}$oz red persimmon, finely chopped
5ml/1 tsp sesame seeds

1 Thinly slice the bamboo shoots and cut into bitesize pieces. When the soaked shiitake mushrooms have reconstituted and become soft, drain and thinly slice them, discarding the stems.

2 Put the beef slices in a bowl. Add the seasoning ingredients and the shiitake mushrooms, and mix together well, so that the meat is thoroughly coated.

3 Heat 15ml/1 tbsp of the vegetable oil in a frying pan over medium heat. Stir-fry the seasoned beef and mushrooms until cooked, then remove from the pan, cool and chill in the refrigerator.

4 Trim the beansprouts and blanch gently in boiling water for 3 minutes. Drain. Blanch the bamboo shoots for about 3 minutes. Drain.

5 In a bowl combine all the dressing ingredients and mix well. Set aside.

6 Beat the egg and season with a pinch of salt. Coat a frying pan with the remaining vegetable oil and heat over medium heat. Add the beaten egg and make a thin omelette, browning gently on each side. Remove from the pan and cut into thin strips.

7 Arrange the beef on a serving plate with the bamboo shoots, watercress or rocket, and beansprouts. Garnish with the sliced chilli and egg strips before serving.

Per portion Energy 268kcal/1115kJ; Protein 17g; Carbohydrate 9.1g, of which sugars 6.1g; Fat 18.6g, of which saturates 3.6g; Cholesterol 119mg; Calcium 164mg; Fibre 3.5g; Sodium 2489mg.

Although *kimchi* is characteristically a cold dish, this stir-fried version gives the vegetables a delicate quality and subtle flavour. The pungent flavour of the raw *kimchi* is removed by the cooking, and replaced by a nutty sweetness that works perfectly with a simple accompaniment of steamed rice.
Serves 2–3

Stir-fried kimchi

150g/5oz cabbage *kimchi*
50g/2oz pork
15ml/1 tbsp vegetable oil
2 garlic cloves, finely chopped
1 spring onion (scallion), sliced

5ml/1 tsp dark soy sauce
2.5ml/$\frac{1}{2}$ tsp sesame seeds
5ml/1 tsp sesame oil
2.5ml/$\frac{1}{2}$ tsp sugar
steamed rice or noodles in broth, to serve

1 Slice the cabbage *kimchi* into 2cm/$\frac{3}{4}$in lengths, and roughly chop the pork into similar sized pieces.

2 Coat a pan with the vegetable oil and stir-fry the garlic until lightly browned. Add the pork and stir-fry until crisp and golden. Drain off any excess oil.

3 Add the *kimchi* and stir-fry for one minute or until the *kimchi* has darkened. Add the spring onion, soy sauce, sesame seeds, sesame oil and sugar, and quickly stir-fry, ensuring all the ingredients are well mixed.

4 Serve immediately, accompanied by steamed rice or a dish of noodles in broth.

Seafood and vegetarian kimchi Shrimps can be used in place of the pork, or for a vegetarian alternative, leave out the meat entirely.

Per portion Energy 84kcal/348kJ; Protein 4.7g; Carbohydrate 2.9g, of which sugars 2.9g; Fat 6g, of which saturates 0.9g; Cholesterol 11mg; Calcium 36mg; Fibre 1.3g; Sodium 135mg.

The mild flavours of stir-fried cabbage *kimchi* are a perfect complement to the delicate taste of blanched tofu. The hint of sweetness and underlying spiciness in the *kimchi* contrasts with the smooth, creamy texture and soybean nuttiness of the tofu. **Serves 3–4**

Tofu & stir-fried kimchi

90g/3½oz cabbage *kimchi*
50g/2oz pork
15ml/1 tbsp vegetable oil
1 garlic clove, thinly sliced
5ml/1 tsp salt

5ml/1 tsp sugar
5ml/1 tsp sesame seeds
5ml/1 tsp sesame oil
1 block firm tofu

1 Slice the *kimchi* into 2cm/¾in lengths, and roughly chop the pork into similar sized pieces.

2 Coat a pan or wok with the vegetable oil and stir-fry the pork and garlic until crisp and golden. Season with the salt.

3 Stir in the *kimchi* and quickly stir-fry over high heat until it has become a dark brown. Add the sugar, sesame seeds and sesame oil. Combine well and stir-fry for a further 30 seconds. Remove from the heat and cover with a lid.

4 Meanwhile place the whole block of tofu into a pan of boiling water, ensuring that it is covered. Boil for 3–4 minutes, and then remove. Drain the tofu, and blot any excess water with kitchen paper. Cut into slices 1cm/½in thick.

5 Arrange the warm tofu slices on a large plate, and place the pork and kimchi mixture in the middle to serve.

For vegetarians Instead of the pork, half a finely chopped onion can be used for a vegetarian alternative.

Per portion Energy 98kcal/407kJ; Protein 7g; Carbohydrate 2.5g, of which sugars 2.3g; Fat 6.7g, of which saturates 1g; Cholesterol 8mg; Calcium 257mg; Fibre 0.6g; Sodium 504mg.

Soybean paste stew

½ courgette (zucchini)
25g/1oz enoki mushrooms
15ml/1 tbsp sesame oil, plus
  extra for drizzling
50g/2oz beef, finely chopped
30ml/2 tbsp *doenjang* soybean
  paste
¼ onion, finely chopped
10ml/2 tsp finely chopped
  garlic
550ml/18fl oz/2½ cups fish
  stock
1 red chilli, seeded and sliced
  diagonally
¼ block firm tofu, diced
1 spring onion (scallion), sliced,
  to garnish

Per portion Energy 166kcal/690kJ; Protein
13g; Carbohydrate 4.8g, of which sugars
3.2g; Fat 10.7g, of which saturates 2.2g;
Cholesterol 15mg; Calcium 169mg; Fibre
3.1g; Sodium 25mg.

Although this rich stew, called *doenjang chige*, has the same fermented soybean paste foundation as many soups, it is an altogether thicker and heartier casserole. The slow cooking imparts a deep, complex flavour full of spiciness. It is a satisfyingly warm dish, ideal for cold winter evenings, and particularly suits the flavour of flame-grilled meat as an accompaniment. **Serves 2**

1 Thickly slice the courgette, and then cut the slices into quarters. Discard the caps from the enoki mushrooms.

2 In a casserole dish or heavy pan, heat the sesame oil over high heat. Add the beef and soybean paste to the pan, and cook until golden brown. Then add the onion and garlic to the pan and sauté gently. Add the fish stock and bring to the boil.

3 Then add the chillies and courgette slices, and boil for 5 minutes. Add the tofu and mushrooms, and boil for a further 2 minutes. Reduce the heat and simmer the stew gently for 15 minutes.

4 Garnish with sliced spring onion and a drizzle of sesame oil, and serve.

Cook's tips
• When making fish stock, you can use stock (bouillon) cubes for convenience, but it is easy to make an authentic fish stock from scratch. Simply simmer a handful of dried anchovies in 1 litre/1¾ pints/4 cups water for approximately 30 minutes, and then strain the stock into a jug (pitcher).
• This dish is traditionally cooked in a heavy stone pot known as a *tukbaege*, although a heavy pan or casserole will work equally well. Serving the dish in the heavy cooking pot ensures that the dish remains warm and continues to cook once it is on the table.
• Enoki mushrooms are available at most Asian stores and are also sometimes found in supermarkets under the name of snow puff mushrooms.

An easy accompaniment for a main course, or a great appetizer. Squares of fried tofu stuffed with a blend of chilli and chestnut give a piquant jolt to the delicate flavour. The tofu has a crispy coating, surrounding a creamy texture, with a crunchy filling. **Serves 2**

Stuffed pan-fried tofu

2 blocks firm tofu
30ml/2 tbsp Thai fish sauce
5ml/1 tsp sesame oil
2 eggs
7.5ml/1½ tsp cornflour
  (cornstarch)
vegetable oil, for shallow-
  frying

For the filling
2 green chillies, finely
  chopped
2 chestnuts, finely chopped
6 garlic cloves, crushed
10ml/2 tsp sesame seeds

1 Cut the block of tofu into 2cm/¾in slices, and then cut each slice in half. Place the tofu slices on a piece of kitchen paper to absorb any excess water.

2 Mix together the Thai fish sauce and sesame oil. Transfer the tofu slices to a plate and coat them with the fish sauce mixture. Leave to marinate for 20 minutes. Meanwhile, put all the filling ingredients into a bowl and combine them thoroughly. Set aside.

3 Beat the egg in a shallow dish. Add the cornflour and whisk until well combined. Take the slices of tofu and dip them into the beaten egg mixture, ensuring an even coating on all sides.

4 Place a frying pan over medium heat and add the vegetable oil. Add the tofu slices to the pan and sauté, turning over once, until golden brown.

5 Once cooked, make a slit down the middle of each slice with a sharp knife, without cutting all the way through. Gently stuff a large pinch of the filling into each slice, and serve.

Per portion Energy 291kcal/1213kJ; Protein 23g; Carbohydrate 7.8g, of which sugars 1.3g; Fat 19.1g, of which saturates 3.4g; Cholesterol 209mg; Calcium 1014mg; Fibre 0.8g; Sodium 88mg.

The underlying fiery spiciness of this dish, called *sundubu chige*, emphasizes its seafood flavours. Clams and prawns are served in a piquant soup with a medley of vegetables, with creamy tofu melting into the rich sauce. **Serves 2–3**

Spicy soft tofu stew

1 block soft tofu
15ml/1 tbsp light soy sauce
6 prawns (shrimp)
6 clams
25g/1oz enoki mushrooms
15ml/1 tbsp vegetable oil
50g/2oz beef, finely chopped
7.5ml/1½ tsp Korean chilli
  powder

5ml/1 tsp crushed garlic
500ml/17fl oz/generous 2
  cups water or beef stock
⅓ leek, sliced
½ red chilli, sliced
½ green chilli, sliced
2.5ml/½ tsp dark soy sauce
1.5ml/¼ tsp Thai fish sauce
salt

1 Break the tofu into small pieces, place in a bowl and marinate with the light soy sauce and a pinch of salt for 1 hour.

2 Hold each prawn between two fingers and gently pull off the tail shell. Twist off the head. Peel away the soft body shell and the small claws beneath. Rinse well. Scrub the clams in cold running water. Discard the caps from the enoki mushrooms.

3 In a flameproof casserole dish or heavy pan, heat the vegetable oil over high heat. Add the chopped beef and stir-fry until the meat has browned. Then add the chilli powder, garlic and a splash of water. Quickly stir-fry, coating the meat with the spices. Add the water or stock and bring to the boil. Add the clams, prawns and tofu, and boil for a further 4 minutes.

4 Reduce the heat slightly and add the leek, chillies and mushrooms. Continue to cook until the leek has softened. Then stir in the dark soy sauce and Thai fish sauce. Season with salt if necessary, and serve.

Per portion Energy 170kcal/709kJ; Protein 21.4g; Carbohydrate 2.1g, of which sugars 1.5g; Fat 8.4g, of which saturates 1.5g; Cholesterol 140mg; Calcium 378mg; Fibre 0.8g; Sodium 734mg.

The silky consistency of the tofu absorbs the dark smoky taste of the soy dressing in this rich and flavourful dish. Tofu has a nutty quality that blends agreeably with the salty sweetness of the soy sauce and the hints of garlic and spring onion. **Serves 2**

Blanched tofu with soy dressing

2 blocks firm tofu
salt

For the dressing
10ml/2 tsp finely sliced
 spring onion (scallion)

5ml/1 tsp finely chopped
 garlic
60ml/4 tbsp dark soy sauce
10ml/2 tsp chilli powder
5ml/1 tsp sugar
10ml/2 tsp sesame seeds

1 To make the dressing, mix the spring onion and garlic in a bowl with the soy sauce, chilli powder, sugar and sesame seeds. Leave the dressing to stand for a few minutes, allowing the flavours to mingle.

2 Meanwhile, bring a large pan of water to the boil, and add a pinch of salt. Place the whole blocks of tofu in the water, being careful not to let them break apart.

3 Blanch the tofu for 3 minutes. Remove and place on kitchen paper to remove any excess water.

4 Transfer the tofu to a plate, and cover with the dressing. Serve, slicing the tofu as desired.

Tofu Koreans traditionally eat this dish without slicing the tofu, preferring instead to either eat it directly with a spoon or pick it apart with chopsticks. It may be easier, however, to slice it in advance if you are serving it as an accompanying dish.

Per portion Energy 160kcal/669kJ; Protein 16.1g; Carbohydrate 6.7g, of which sugars 5.6g; Fat 7.8g, of which saturates 0.9g; Cholesterol 0mg; Calcium 954mg; Fibre 0.1g; Sodium 2144mg.

This chilled noodle salad, called *bibim naengmyun*, is ideal for a summer lunch dish. The cool temperature of the buckwheat noodles contrasts with the spiciness of the dressing, and Asian pear adds a delicious sweetness.
Serves 2

Spicy buckwheat noodles

90g/3½oz *naengmyun* buckwheat noodles
1 hard-boiled egg
½ cucumber
½ Asian pear
ice cubes, to serve

For the sauce
30ml/2 tbsp *gochujang* chilli paste
5ml/1 tsp Korean chilli powder
30ml/2 tbsp sugar
10ml/2 tsp sesame oil
1 garlic clove, finely chopped
2.5ml/½ tsp soy sauce
5ml/1 tsp sesame seeds

1 Cook the noodles in a large pan of boiling water for 5 minutes. Drain them, and then rinse two or three times in cold water until the water runs clear. Chill for 30 minutes.

2 Slice the hard-boiled egg in half. Seed the cucumber and slice it into long, thin matchstick strips. Peel and core the Asian pear and slice it into fine matchstick strips.

3 In a large bowl combine all the ingredients for the sauce and blend well together. Arrange the noodles in the centre of a large serving platter. Pour over the sauce and then sprinkle with the julienne pear and cucumber. Place the egg on the top and add ice cubes to the plate before serving.

Naengmyun noodles Be sure to use a large pan with plenty of water when cooking *naengmyun* noodles, as they contain a lot of starch so will stick to the pan and each other easily. Add a few drops of oil while cooking to help keep them separate.

Per portion Energy 337kcal/1421kJ; Protein 9.4g; Carbohydrate 58.3g, of which sugars 25.1g; Fat 9g, of which saturates 1.3g; Cholesterol 105mg; Calcium 52mg; Fibre 3.3g; Sodium 133mg.

Blanching, fermentation and spicy dressings

 Korean table settings traditionally rely on a range of dishes shared between all the diners. However, there are some dishes that are served in individual portions to each person, and these comprise the heart of every Korean meal. Rice and soup are always present on the table – even at breakfast – but it is the vegetable accompaniments that vary from meal to meal throughout the year, and add a special character to even the simplest of repasts.

While rice and soup will remain customarily unchanged from season to season, the vegetables that make up a meal will vary depending on what is readily available. As with the cuisine of every country, Korean cooking enjoys recipes that make the most of the seasonal variation in fresh produce, and turn the ingredients into a dish suited to the weather and other fare on offer. These dishes are known as *sangchae* and comprise one half of the vegetable accompaniment dishes in Korean cuisine, the other half being *namul* recipes.

Sangchae uses fresh vegetables coated in a spicy dressing, and makes for tangy, crunchy dishes. The ingredients are dictated by the weather and harvest, and while spring dishes may rely on the light refreshing qualities of cucumber and chive *sangchae*, the autumnal harvest table instead favours the earthier, nutty tastes of the white radish variant that brings warmth from a combination of cider vinegar and red chilli paste.

In contrast, *namul* dishes are much milder, instead using a simple dressing of sesame oil, garlic, rice wine and dark soy sauce. *Namul* dishes have a more delicate flavour, and the vegetables are blanched first to create a softer texture without losing any of the valuable nutrients.

Both *sangchae* and *namul* dishes are made up of just one vegetable, as the flavours are considered more natural and organic if the different vegetables are not mixed together.

In both cases the intrinsic tastes and textures of the vegetables are preserved in the Korean method of cooking, and despite the seasonings adding their spicy or nutty qualities, the fresh flavours of the vegetables come through robustly.

However, no Korean meal is truly complete without the national dish of *kimchi*. Vegetables are seasoned, sealed and left to ferment, creating a unique flavour that has a fiery kick of red chilli. Hints of garlic permeate, and the pickling process creates an unmistakably sour edge. The fermentation leaves the vegetables with a softened texture, and yet they retain their crunch in the mouth.

Korea boasts more than a hundred types of *kimchi*, all rich in vitamins and minerals, and its production is a challenging and revered art. Kinds vary according to which vegetables are in season, and also to the region of production. The summer yields cooling cucumber *kimchi*, while winter gives way to a heartier pickled cabbage variety better suited to the dishes of the season. A ubiquitous favourite when cold, and a classic staple of every meal, *kimchi* is also regularly blended into cooked dishes to capitalize on its unique flavour.

The sweet, slightly vinegary taste of Chinese white radish provides a refreshing foundation to this healthy dish. The red chilli and sesame oil dressing adds an understated spiciness and nutty aftertaste. The white radish, also known as *daikon*, is a commonly used ingredient in Asian cooking and is valued for its medicinal properties. **Serves 2**

White radish sangchae

225g/8oz Chinese white
  radish, peeled
¼ red chilli, shredded, and
  1.5ml/¼ tsp sesame seeds,
  to garnish

For the marinade
5ml/1 tsp cider vinegar
2.5ml/½ tsp sugar
1.5ml/¼ tsp salt
7.5ml/1½ tsp lemon juice
2.5ml/½ tsp Korean chilli
  powder

1 Cut the radish into thin strips approximately 5cm/2in long.

2 To make the marinade, mix the vinegar, sugar, salt, lemon juice and chilli powder together in a small bowl, ensuring the ingredients are thoroughly blended.

3 Place the radish in a bowl, and add the marinade. Leave to marinate for 20 minutes, then place in the refrigerator until the dish has chilled thoroughly.

4 Garnish with the shredded chilli pepper and sesame seeds before serving.

Variation The radish will take on some of the red colour of the chilli powder, but for an interesting alternative try replacing the chilli powder with 2.5ml/½ tsp wasabi. This will give a green tint and a sharper taste.

Per portion Energy 22kcal/91kJ; Protein 1g; Carbohydrate 3.2g, of which sugars 3.2g; Fat 0.7g, of which saturates 0.2g; Cholesterol 0mg; Calcium 27mg; Fibre 1.1g; Sodium 209mg.

Cucumber sangchae

The refreshing, succulent taste of this simple salad makes a perfect accompaniment for a main meal on a hot summer's night. Small pickling cucumbers are the best for this dish; they are not as watery as the larger specimens and they do not require peeling. **Serves 2**

400g/14oz pickling or salad
  cucumber
30ml/2 tbsp salt

For the dressing
2 spring onions (scallions),
  finely chopped
2 garlic cloves, crushed

5ml/1 tsp cider vinegar
5ml/1 tsp salt
3ml/½ tsp Korean chilli powder
10ml/2 tsp toasted sesame seeds
10ml/2 tsp sesame oil
5ml/1 tsp *gochujang* chilli paste
10ml/2 tsp sugar

1 Cut the cucumber lengthways into thin slices and put into a colander. Sprinkle with the salt, mix well and leave for 30 minutes.

2 Place the cucumber slices in a damp dish towel and gently squeeze out as much of the water as possible.

3 Place the spring onions in a large bowl. Add the crushed garlic, vinegar, salt and chilli powder, and stir to combine. Sprinkle in the sesame seeds and mix in the sesame oil, chilli paste and sugar.

4 Blend the cucumber with the dressing. Chill before serving.

Per portion Energy 105kcal/432kJ; Protein 3.3g; Carbohydrate 9.2g, of which sugars 7.4g; Fat 6.2g, of which saturates 0.9g; Cholesterol 0mg; Calcium 78mg; Fibre 2.2g; Sodium 1973mg.

Korean chive sangchae

The Korean chive has a garlic nuance in both taste and aroma, and the leaves have a soft, grasslike texture. This dish is the perfect accompaniment for any grilled meat, and is a tasty alternative to the classic shredded spring onion salad. **Serves 2**

200g/7oz fresh Korean or
  Chinese chives
1 green chilli, seeded and finely
  sliced
10ml/2 tsp sesame seeds, to
  garnish

For the seasoning
30ml/2 tbsp dark soy sauce
2 garlic cloves, crushed
10ml/2 tsp Korean chilli powder
10ml/2 tsp sesame oil
10ml/2 tsp sugar

1 Clean the chives, then trim off the bulbs and discard. Slice roughly into 4cm/1½in lengths. Combine with the chilli in a bowl.

2 To make the seasoning, mix the soy sauce, garlic, chilli powder, sesame oil and sugar together, and then add it to the bowl with the chives and chilli. Mix until well coated, then chill.

3 Garnish with sesame seeds and serve.

Spring onion sangchae For a traditional alternative use 150g/5oz shredded spring onion (scallion) in place of the chives, and add 15ml/1 tbsp cider vinegar and 15ml/1 tbsp soy sauce to the seasoning.

Per portion Energy 105Kcal/434kJ; Protein 4.3g; Carbohydrate 7g, of which sugars 6.7g; Fat 6.7g, of which saturates 0.9g; Cholesterol 0mg; Calcium 196mg; Fibre 2.3g; Sodium 1196mg.

White radish namul

This subtle dish blends the sweetness of white radish with a delicious nutty aftertaste. Blanching the white radish softens it, leaving it with a silky texture. **Serves 2**

400g/14oz Chinese white
  radish, peeled
50g/2oz leek, finely sliced
20ml/4 tsp sesame oil, plus
  extra for drizzling

5ml/1 tsp salt
60ml/4 tbsp vegetable oil
½ red chilli, seeded and finely
  shredded, to garnish

1 Slice the radish into 5cm/2in matchstick lengths. Blanch in a pan of boiling water for 30 seconds. Drain, and gently squeeze to remove any excess water.

2 Mix the leek with the sesame oil and salt in a large bowl.

3 Place a pan over medium heat, and add the vegetable oil. Add the radish, and sauté gently for 1 minute. Add the leek mixture, and sauté for a further 2 minutes. Remove from the heat and garnish with the shredded chilli and a drizzle of sesame oil before serving.

Per portion Energy 137kcal/565kJ; Protein 1.8g; Carbohydrate 4.5g, of which sugars 4.3g; Fat 12.5g, of which saturates 1.8g; Cholesterol 0mg; Calcium 45mg; Fibre 2.4g; Sodium 1005mg.

Spinach namul

Using the stems as well as the leaves of the spinach gives a subtle crunch to complement the smooth texture of the greens. The hint of bitterness in the spinach is offset by the salty soy sauce. **Serves 2**

500g/18oz spinach
60ml/4 tbsp dark soy sauce
2 small garlic cloves, crushed
20ml/4 tsp sesame oil
3ml/½ tsp rice wine

20ml/4 tsp sesame seeds
30ml/2 tbsp vegetable oil
salt

1 Trim the ends of the spinach stalks. Cut the leaves and stalks into 10cm/4in lengths. Boil the spinach in a pan of lightly salted water for 30 seconds. Drain, and rinse under cold running water.

2 Mix the soy sauce, garlic, sesame oil and rice wine together in a large bowl. Add the spinach and coat the leaves and stems with the seasoning mixture. In a dry pan lightly toast the sesame seeds until golden brown, then set aside.

3 Heat the vegetable oil in a frying pan or wok, and sauté the spinach over high heat for 20 seconds. Transfer to a serving dish and garnish with the toasted sesame seeds before serving.

Per portion Energy 293kcal/1208kJ; Protein 10.1g; Carbohydrate 7.4g, of which sugars 6.1g; Fat 24.8g, of which saturates 3.2g; Cholesterol 0mg; Calcium 499mg; Fibre 6.2g; Sodium 2488mg.

Cucumber namul

Soya beansprout namul

This sautéed dish retains the natural succulence of the cucumber, while also infusing the recipe with a pleasantly refreshing hint of garlic and chilli. **Serves 2**

The delicate spiciness of the red chilli and nutty flavour of the sesame oil creates a tantalizing and crunchy dish. Crispy soya beansprouts can be replaced with mung beansprouts. **Serves 2**

200g/7oz cucumber
15ml/1 tbsp vegetable oil
5ml/1 tsp spring onion
 (scallion), finely chopped
1 garlic clove, crushed

5ml/1 tsp sesame oil
sesame seeds, and seeded and
 shredded red chilli, to garnish
salt

300g/10oz/generous 1 cup
 soya beansprouts
60ml/4 tbsp vegetable oil
$\frac{2}{3}$ red chilli, seeded and
 sliced

1 baby leek, finely sliced
10ml/2 tsp sesame oil
salt

1 Thinly slice the cucumber and place in a colander. Sprinkle with salt, then leave to stand for 10 minutes. Drain off any excess liquid and transfer to a clean bowl.

2 Coat a frying pan or wok with the vegetable oil, and heat it over medium heat. Add the spring onion, garlic and cucumber, and quickly stir-fry together.

3 Remove from the heat, add the sesame oil and toss lightly to blend the ingredients. Place in a shallow serving dish and garnish with the sesame seeds and shredded chilli before serving.

1 Wash the soya beansprouts, and trim the tail ends. Cover them with a light sprinkling of salt, and leave to stand for 10 minutes.

2 Bring a pan of water to the boil, and add the beansprouts. Cover and boil for 3 minutes, then drain.

3 Place a frying pan or wok over medium heat and add the vegetable oil. Add the soya beansprouts, and sauté gently for 30 seconds. Add the chilli and leek, and stir-fry together so that the ingredients are thoroughly blended.

4 Transfer to a shallow dish and drizzle with a little sesame oil before serving.

Per portion Energy 74kcal/304kJ; Protein 0.8g; Carbohydrate 1.7g, of which sugars 1.6g; Fat 7.1g, of which saturates 0.9g; Cholesterol 0mg; Calcium 20mg; Fibre 0.7g; Sodium 4mg.

Per portion Energy 282kcal/1167kJ; Protein 5.2g; Carbohydrate 7.5g, of which sugars 4.4g; Fat 26g, of which saturates 3.2g; Cholesterol 0mg; Calcium 42mg; Fibre 3.4g; Sodium 9mg.

The fresh taste of the courgette in this *namul* dish mingles with the flavours of sesame oil and a hint of seafood in the form of shrimp. The dried shrimp gives a pleasing crunchiness, which contrasts nicely with the texture of the courgette.
Serves 2

Courgette namul

2 courgettes (zucchini),
  finely sliced
10ml/2 tsp sesame oil
30ml/2 tbsp vegetable oil
2 garlic cloves, crushed

40g/1½oz dried shrimp
finely chopped spring onion
  (scallion) and sesame
  seeds, to garnish
salt

1 Place the courgette slices in a colander, lightly sprinkle them with salt and leave to stand for 20 minutes. Drain off any excess liquid and transfer to a bowl.

2 Add the sesame oil to the courgette slices and mix together to coat.

3 Coat a frying pan or wok with the vegetable oil and heat over high heat. Add the seasoned courgettes and crushed garlic, and stir-fry briefly. Add the dried shrimp and stir-fry quickly until they become crispy, but the courgettes should retain their bright green colour.

4 Remove from the heat, and transfer to a shallow dish. Garnish with the spring onion, and sprinkle over the sesame seeds before serving.

Dried shrimp You will find dried shrimp at most Asian stores. Chopped fresh prawns (shrimp) can be substituted as an alternative; they will provide a similar flavour, although not the same crunchy texture.

Per portion Energy 213kcal/883kJ; Protein 15g; Carbohydrate 3.9g, of which sugars 3.7g; Fat 15.3g, of which saturates 2g; Cholesterol 101mg; Calcium 294mg; Fibre 2g; Sodium 869mg.

In this tempting *namul* dish the distinctive taste of sesame oil emphasizes the rich and meaty flavour of the shiitake mushrooms. The mushrooms are quickly sautéed to soften them as well as to accentuate their characteristic earthy flavours. **Serves 2**

Shiitake mushroom namul

12 dried shiitake mushrooms, soaked in warm water for about 30 minutes until softened
10ml/2 tsp sesame seeds
2 garlic cloves, crushed

30ml/2 tbsp vegetable oil
½ spring onion (scallion), finely chopped
10ml/2 tsp sesame oil
salt

1 When the soaked shiitake mushrooms have reconstituted and become soft, drain and slice them, discarding the stems, and then place them in a bowl. Add the sesame seeds, crushed garlic and a pinch of salt, and blend the ingredients together.

2 Coat a frying pan or wok with the vegetable oil and place over high heat. Add the seasoned mushroom slices and quickly stir-fry them, so that they soften slightly but do not lose their firmness.

3 Remove from the heat and stir in the spring onion and sesame oil. Transfer to a shallow dish and serve.

Cook's tip
• It is important to drain the shiitake mushrooms thoroughly to ensure that their dark colour does not overwhelm the dish. Try squeezing the mushrooms gently to remove all the liquid, and then pat dry with kitchen paper.

Per portion Energy 167kcal/689kJ; Protein 2.2g; Carbohydrate 1.1g, of which sugars 0.2g; Fat 17.2g, of which saturates 2.2g; Cholesterol 0mg; Calcium 38mg; Fibre 1.2g; Sodium 4mg.

Classic cabbage kimchi

The classic variety of *kimchi*, and one most likely to be found at any meal, is made with crispy white Chinese leaves. The leaves are stained a vibrant red with chilli powder, and speckled with crushed garlic and ginger. The spiciness of the chilli contrasts with salty seafood flavours and a hint of tangy spring onion. This dish takes a minimum of two days to prepare. **Serves 10**

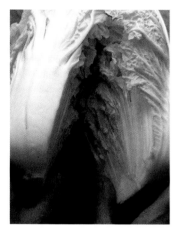  

1 head Chinese leaves (Chinese cabbage), about 2kg/4½lb
salt

For the marinade
50g/2oz/½ cup coarse sea salt
75ml/5 tbsp water
30ml/2 tbsp table salt

For the seasoning
2 oysters (optional)
½ Chinese white radish, about 500g/1¼lb, peeled and thinly sliced
25g/1oz Korean chives
25g/1oz *minari*, watercress or rocket (arugula)
5 garlic cloves
15g/½oz fresh root ginger, peeled
½ onion
½ Asian pear, or ½ kiwi fruit
1 chestnut, sliced
3 spring onions (scallions), sliced
50g/2oz/½ cup Korean chilli powder
120ml/4fl oz/½ cup Thai fish sauce
5ml/1 tsp sugar
1 red chilli, sliced

1 Make a deep cut across the base of the head of Chinese leaves and split it into two by hand. Repeat with the two halves, splitting them into quarters. Place the quartered head in a bowl and cover with water, adding 30ml/2 tbsp salt. Leave to soak for 2 hours.

2 Drain the cabbage and sprinkle with the sea salt for the marinade, making sure to coat between the leaves. Leave to stand for 4 hours.

3 Hold an oyster with the rounded shell up. Push the tip of an oyster knife or short-bladed knife into the hinge of the oyster and twist to prise the shell open. Cut the two muscles inside. Run the blade between the shells to open them. Cut the oyster away from the flat shell. Repeat with the other oyster. Season with a pinch of salt.

4 Cut the radish slices into fine strips. Cut the chives and *minari*, watercress or rocket into 5cm/2in lengths. Finely chop or blend the garlic, ginger, onion and Asian pear or kiwi fruit. Mix all the seasoning ingredients together in a large bowl with 120ml/4fl oz/½ cup water.

5 Rinse the softened quarters of Chinese leaves in cold running water. Place in a large bowl and coat with the seasoning mixture, ensuring that the mixture gets between the leaves and that no leaf is left uncovered.

6 The outermost leaf of each quarter of cabbage will have softened, and can be wrapped tightly around the other leaves to help the seasoning permeate throughout.

7 Place the Chinese leaves in an airtight container. Leave to stand at room temperature for 5 hours, then leave in the refrigerator for 24 hours.

Cook's Tips
• *Kimchi* can be stored for up to five months in the refrigerator. The flavour may then be too pungent to eat raw, but the *kimchi* can be used for cooked dishes.
• Wear plastic gloves when coating the Chinese leaves with the seasoning, to prevent your hands becoming stained by the chilli powder.
• *Minari*, also known as Japanese parsley, is available from any Asian food store.

Per portion Energy 73kcal/303kJ; Protein 3.6g; Carbohydrate 13.5g, of which sugars 12.9g; Fat 0.6g, of which saturates 0.1g; Cholesterol 0mg; Calcium 121mg; Fibre 5.1g; Sodium 383mg.

A classic summer variety of *kimchi*, the refreshing natural succulence of cucumber is perfect on a hot, humid day. The spiciness of the chilli is neutralized by the moistness of the cucumber, with flavours that invigorate the palate. **Serves 4**

Stuffed cucumber kimchi

15 small pickling cucumbers
30ml/2 tbsp sea salt
1 bunch Chinese chives

For the seasoning
1 onion
4 spring onions (scallions), thinly sliced
75ml/5 tbsp Korean chilli powder

15ml/1 tbsp Thai fish sauce
10ml/2 tsp salt
1 garlic clove, crushed
7.5ml/1$\frac{1}{2}$ tsp grated fresh root ginger
5ml/1 tsp sugar
5ml/1 tsp sesame seeds

1 If the cucumbers are long, cut them in half widthways. Make two slits in a cross down the length of each cucumber or cucumber half, making sure not to cut all the way to the end. Coat thoroughly with the sea salt, and leave for 1 hour.

2 Cut the Chinese chives into 2.5cm/1in lengths, discarding the bulb.

3 Combine the onion and spring onions with the Chinese chives in a bowl. Add 45ml/3 tbsp of the chilli powder and add the Thai fish sauce, salt, garlic, ginger, sugar and sesame seeds. Mix the ingredients thoroughly by hand, using plastic gloves to prevent the chilli powder from staining your skin.

4 Lightly rinse the cucumbers to remove the salt crystals. Coat with the remaining chilli powder, and press the seasoning into the slits. Put the cucumber into an airtight container and leave at room temperature for 12 hours before serving.

Per portion Energy 32kcal/131kJ; Protein 2.5g; Carbohydrate 3.9g, of which sugars 3.4g; Fat 2.1g, of which saturates 0.2g; Cholesterol 0mg; Calcium 88mg; Fibre 1.4g; Sodium 2067mg.

White radish *kimchi* is traditionally eaten as the autumn evenings start to draw in, with a spiciness that fortifies against the cold. The pungent aromas and tangy flavours make this one of the most popular *kimchi* varieties.
Serves 4

Diced white radish kimchi

1.5kg/3½lb Chinese white radish, peeled
225g/8oz/2 cups coarse sea salt
5ml/1 tsp sugar

For the seasoning
75ml/5 tbsp Korean chilli powder
1 garlic clove, crushed

¼ onion, finely chopped
3 spring onions (scallions), finely sliced
15ml/1 tbsp sea salt
5ml/1 tsp Thai fish sauce
5ml/1 tsp fresh root ginger, peeled and finely chopped
22.5ml/4½ tsp light muscovado (brown) sugar

1 Cut the radish into 2cm/¾in cubes. Place in a bowl and coat with the sea salt. Leave for 2 hours, draining off any water that collects at the bottom of the bowl.

2 Combine all the ingredients for the seasoning and mix well with the salted radish. Place the radish in an airtight container and seal. Leave at room temperature for 24 hours and chill before serving.

Spice it up For extra kick add a finely chopped red chilli to the seasoning, but be warned, this will make the dish extremely hot.

Tangy and sweet Blend half an onion in a food processor and add it to the seasoning for a tangier taste and subtle sweetness.

Per portion Energy 73kcal/302kJ; Protein 3.1g; Carbohydrate 14g, of which sugars 13.6g; Fat 0.8g, of which saturates 0.4g; Cholesterol 0mg; Calcium 81mg; Fibre 3.7g; Sodium 1203mg.

Tempting delights: flower petals and ice flakes

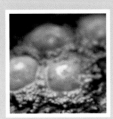

Despite the relatively limited number of Korean desserts, there are some wonderful sweet dishes that use deliciously unexpected ingredients.

In the dish of *baesuk* poached pears are given a lift when flavoured with whole peppercorns, creating a tantalizing combination of sweetness and spice. *Kyungdan* sweet rice balls are filled with bean paste and then covered in a mixture of red dates, chestnuts and sesame seeds to produce a crunchy coating that gives way to a wonderfully light and fluffy centre.

However, arguably the most popular national confectionery is a refreshing chilled sweet called crunchy ice flakes. These are coated with a purée of red beans and maple syrup, and then topped with fresh fruit. As commonplace in Korea as ice cream, this exotic dish makes for a wonderful frozen treat.

Sweet rice cakes and delicate cookies are popular as desserts too, although with these dishes the appearance is arguably as important as the taste. The traditional wafer-thin *maejakgwa* contain crushed pumpkin, apricot and seaweed for beautiful pastel shades of yellow, pink and green. Likewise, *hwachun* rice cakes in honey dressing have flower petals pressed into the surface to create both an intriguing flavour and a dessert which looks as good as it tastes.

Whereas sweet dishes were historically reserved for the banqueting tables of royalty and the upper classes, in contemporary Korea they have become much more widely used and are now eaten on a range of occasions. Weddings and the advent of the New Year are celebrated with fragrant confectionery, and sweet chilled punch is enjoyed during the summer.

Indeed, a glass of punch is a more popular way to finish a meal in Korea, and a bowl of sweet rice punch with ice cubes floating on the surface is wonderfully refreshing on a hot day. For a more spicy variation, the traditional Korean punch made from dried persimmons and root ginger is a perfect autumn alternative, and has lovely warmth combined with a rich fruitiness.

There are a number of classic sweets as well, which are eaten throughout the year. The most popular is *yakwa*: sweet cinnamon, ginger and sake cookies served with green tea to finish a meal. Although fresh fruit forms the traditional end to a meal, Korean cuisine has a superb assortment of delightful, tempting desserts with distinctive flavours.

This non-alcoholic punch is a popular dessert in Korea. The sweetness of the dried persimmons is matched by the sharpness of the cinnamon, and the dish has a refreshing fruit kick that makes it the perfect way to finish a spicy meal.
Serves 4

Persimmon & ginger punch

12 dried persimmons
12 walnuts
150g/5oz fresh root ginger, peeled and thinly sliced
1 cinnamon stick
450g/1lb/2 cups light muscovado brown sugar
30ml/2 tbsp maple syrup or golden (light corn) syrup
30 pine nuts

1 Seed the dried persimmons and soak them in cold water until they have softened. Then make an incision into the centre of each, and stuff each one with a walnut. Set aside.

2 Pour 1 litre/1¾ pints/4 cups water into a pan and add the ginger and cinnamon stick. Place over a low heat and simmer gently for 15 minutes, or until the water has taken on the flavour of the ginger and cinnamon. When the liquid has reduced by a fifth to a quarter, strain it through muslin (cheesecloth) into a jug (pitcher). Pour the liquid back into the pan, add the sugar and maple or golden syrup and then bring to the boil again. Remove from the heat and pour into a jug. Cool, then chill in the refrigerator.

3 Place three persimmons in a small serving bowl for each person, and pour over the chilled liquid. Decorate with a sprinkling of pine nuts, and serve.

Per portion Energy 379kcal/1589kJ; Protein 4.9g; Carbohydrate 48.4g, of which sugars 48.3g; Fat 19.8g, of which saturates 1.6g; Cholesterol 0mg; Calcium 47mg; Fibre 1.6g; Sodium 31mg.

A thirst-quenching rice and malt punch, *shikhae* has a lovely sweet taste with a hint of spice. It is the most popular of traditional Korean drinks, particularly on a hot day when nothing beats a bowl of the fragrant chilled liquid with ice cubes floating on top. **Serves 4**

Sweet rice punch

450g/1lb/4 cups malt
350g/12oz/3 cups cooked
  rice
30ml/2 tbsp sugar

10g/¼oz fresh root ginger,
  peeled and sliced
1 cinnamon stick
1 red date, thinly sliced, pine
  nuts, and ice cubes to serve

1 Roughly blend the malt in a food processor, then place in a large bowl. Add 1.5 litres/2½ pints/6¼ cups water and leave for 1 hour. Drain the liquid through muslin (cheesecloth) into a bowl, reserving the malt in the cloth. Repeat this process again, pouring the liquid repeatedly through the malt-lined cloth. After three or four times the liquid should thicken and become opaque. Discard the malt.

2 Put the cooked rice into a large pan and add the malt liquid. Heat gently to 40°C/104°F or hand hot and keep at that temperature for about 5 hours. Once the grains begin to float on the surface remove the rice from the liquid, cool and place in a bowl in the refrigerator.

3 Turn the heat under the malt liquid to high. Once boiling add the sugar, ginger and cinnamon, and simmer for a few minutes. After this discard the ginger and cinnamon stick, and transfer the liquid to a jug (pitcher). Cool and chill in the refrigerator.

4 In a small bowl combine the chilled rice and malt liquid. Add a sprinkling of sliced red date, a handful of pine nuts and some ice cubes before serving.

Per portion Energy 186kcal/791kJ; Protein 3.5g; Carbohydrate 42.5g, of which sugars 8.4g; Fat 1.4g, of which saturates 0.3g; Cholesterol 0mg; Calcium 26mg; Fibre 1.8g; Sodium 2mg.

For this dish, called *baesuk*, Asian pears are poached until tender in liquid swimming with black peppercorns and sliced ginger. It is sweet, but has a delicate spiciness which makes a cleansing and refreshing end to a meal. **Serves 4**

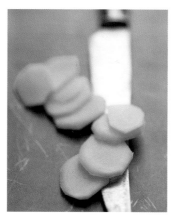  

Poached pear with peppercorns

2 Asian pears
20 black peppercorns
10g/¼oz fresh root ginger, peeled and sliced

25g/1oz/2 tbsp sugar
pine nuts, to decorate

1 Peel and core the Asian pears. Cut into six pieces and press 2 or 3 peppercorns into the smooth outer surface of each piece.

2 Place 750ml/1¼ pints/3 cups water in a large pan and add the ginger. Bring to the boil and cook for 10 minutes, or until the flavour of the ginger has suffused the water. Add the sugar and then the pears. Reduce the heat, and simmer for 5 minutes, or until the pears have softened.

3 Transfer the fruit and liquid to a bowl. Cool, remove the sliced ginger and place the bowl in the refrigerator to chill.

4 To serve, place three pieces of pear into a small bowl for each person, pour over the liquid and decorate with pine nuts.

Variation If Asian pears are not available then Conference pears can be used in their place. However, they should be cored and used whole – one per person – rather than sliced.

Per portion Energy 60kcal/253kJ; Protein 0.3g; Carbohydrate 15.4g, of which sugars 15.4g; Fat 0.1g, of which saturates 0g; Cholesterol 0mg; Calcium 12mg; Fibre 1.7g; Sodium 3mg.

This gorgeous spring dish, called *hwachun*, uses edible flower petals to flavour rice cakes, which are then drizzled with honey. Its sophisticated appearance is matched by its refined, exquisite taste. Serve with a cup of green tea. **Serves 4**

Flower petal rice cakes in honey

20 edible flower petals
225g/8oz/2 cups sweet
  rice flour
2.5ml/½ tsp salt

vegetable oil, for shallow-
  frying
honey, for drizzling

1 Rinse the flower petals, and gently pat them dry with kitchen paper.

2 Sift the flour and salt into a bowl and add 300ml/½ pint/ 1¼ cups warm water. Mix well and knead for 10 minutes. Place on a lightly floured surface and roll out the dough to 1cm/½in thick. Use a floured 5cm/2in biscuit (cookie) cutter to cut the dough into rounds.

3 Heat the oil in a frying pan over a low flame. Add the rice cakes and fry for 2 minutes, or until lightly browned. Flip over and cook on the other side, and then remove from the pan. Place on kitchen paper to drain the excess oil, then arrange on a serving platter.

4 Sprinkle the petals over the rice cakes, and then drizzle with honey.

Edible flowers A number of different flowers have edible petals, including roses, azaleas, apple blossom, carnations and chrysanthemums, and they can sometimes be found at supermarkets or grocery stores.

Per portion Energy 255kcal/1065kJ; Protein 3.6g; Carbohydrate 45.1g, of which sugars 0g; Fat 6g, of which saturates 0.7g; Cholesterol 0mg; Calcium 14mg; Fibre 1.1g; Sodium 249mg.

For *kyungdan*, fluffy rice balls are filled with a delicious sweet bean paste to create a light, succulent dessert. The sweets are coated with red dates, chestnuts and sesame seeds, which give them an unusual texture. The fruit and nuts contrast wonderfully with the meltingly tender rice. **Serves 4**

Sweet rice balls

375g/13oz/2 cups red kidney beans, soaked overnight
200g/7oz/1 cup sugar
30ml/2 tbsp black sesame seeds
20 red dates, stoned (pitted) and finely chopped
20 chestnuts, finely chopped
400g/13oz/3½ cups sweet rice flour
5ml/1 tsp salt

1 Place the beans in a pan, cover with water and bring to the boil. Boil fast for 20 minutes, then drain and leave to cool. Roll them between the palms of your hands to remove the skins. Purée the peeled beans and sugar to a fine paste. Simmer the purée in a pan until the paste resembles a custard consistency.

2 Lightly toast the sesame seeds in a dry pan. Place the dates, chestnuts and sesame seeds in three separate shallow dishes.

3 Sift the flour and salt into a bowl and add 500ml/17fl oz/2¼ cups warm water. Mix well and knead for 10 minutes. Take a small piece of dough, make an indent with your finger and add a little bean paste. Wrap the dough over and form into a ball.

4 Bring a large pan of water to the boil and add the rice balls. Cook for 7 minutes, then drain and rinse in cold water.

5 Separate the rice balls into three groups. Roll one-third in the chopped dates, another in the chestnuts and the last in the toasted sesame seeds. Arrange on a serving platter.

Per portion Energy 973kcal/4111kJ; Protein 30.1g; Carbohydrate 199.9g, of which sugars 66g; Fat 7.9g, of which saturates 1.1g; Cholesterol 0mg; Calcium 224mg; Fibre 19.8g; Sodium 34mg.

For this refreshing, chilled dessert, unique to Korea, crunchy ice flakes are coated with a purée of red beans and maple syrup, and then topped with fresh fruit. This is unquestionably the most popular choice for a hot summer's day. **Serves 2**

Sweet beans on ice flakes

80g/3oz/¹⁄₂ cup red kidney
  beans, soaked overnight
115g/4oz/¹⁄₂ cup sugar
5ml/1 tsp salt
30ml/2 tbsp maple syrup

ice cubes
30ml/2 tbsp condensed milk
90ml/6 tbsp milk
1 kiwi fruit, sliced
2 strawberries

1 Place the red beans in a pan, cover with water and bring to the boil. Boil fast for 10 minutes, then simmer until the beans have softened. Drain and leave to cool, then roll them between the palms of your hands to remove the skins.

2 Put the peeled beans, sugar, salt and maple syrup into a food processor or blender and purée to a fine paste. Put the puréed beans into a pan and simmer until the paste has reduced to the consistency of custard. Cool, then chill.

3 Use an ice crusher, food processor or blender to crush the ice into flakes (you will need 2 litres/3¹⁄₂ pints/8 cups of flakes) and transfer them to a serving bowl. Mix the condensed milk and milk in a jug (pitcher) and pour over the ice flakes in the bowl. Pour the bean paste over the top and decorate with the kiwi fruit and strawberries before serving.

Variations A variety of fruits can be used depending on what is available in season, with blueberries and raspberries making delicious alternatives. A scoop of vanilla ice cream also provides the dish with a richer flavour.

Per portion Energy 462kcal/1968kJ; Protein 11.4g; Carbohydrate 105.1g, of which sugars 88.4g; Fat 2.5g, of which saturates 1.2g; Cholesterol 6mg; Calcium 145mg; Fibre 7g; Sodium 1063mg.

Three-colour ribbon cookies

30ml/2 tbsp pine nuts, finely
    ground
vegetable oil, for deep-frying

For the green cookies
115g/4oz/1 cup plain
    (all-purpose) flour
2.5ml/$\frac{1}{2}$ tsp salt
10g/$\frac{1}{4}$oz grated fresh root
    ginger
30ml/2 tbsp seaweed, finely
    ground

For the yellow cookies
115g/4oz/1 cup plain
    (all-purpose) flour
2.5ml/$\frac{1}{2}$ tsp salt
10g/$\frac{1}{4}$oz grated fresh root
    ginger
50g/2oz sweet pumpkin, finely
    minced (ground)

For the pink cookies
115g/4oz/1 cup plain
    (all-purpose) flour
2.5ml/$\frac{1}{2}$ tsp salt
10g/$\frac{1}{4}$oz grated fresh root
    ginger
50g/2oz apricot flesh, finely
    minced (ground)

For the syrup
250ml/8fl oz/1 cup water
200g/7oz/1 cup sugar
30ml/2 tbsp honey
2.5ml/$\frac{1}{2}$ tsp cinnamon
salt

These delightful ribbon cookies, called *maejakgwa*, look as good as they taste. The crisp twists of wafer-thin dough are tinted in pastel shades of green, yellow and pink, and have a lovely hint of gingery spiciness. These cookies are perfect when served with either a sweet drink or a cup of green tea. **Serves 4**

1 To make the green cookies, sift the flour and salt into a large bowl and mix in the grated ginger, ground seaweed and a splash of water. Knead gently into a smooth, elastic dough. Place on a lightly floured surface and roll out the dough to about 3mm/$\frac{1}{8}$in thick. Cut the dough into strips approximately 2cm/$\frac{3}{4}$in wide and 5cm/2in long.

2 To make the yellow cookies, sift the flour and salt into a large bowl and mix in the grated ginger, minced pumpkin and a splash of water. Continue as for the green cookies.

3 To make the pink cookies, sift the flour and salt into a large bowl and mix in the grated ginger, minced apricot and a splash of water. Continue as for the green cookies.

4 Score three cuts lengthways into each cookie, and bring one end of the strip back through the centre slit to form a loose knot.

5 Put the water, sugar and honey in a pan, and add a pinch of salt. Bring to the boil without stirring, then add the cinnamon and continue to boil, stirring until the syrup becomes sticky. Pour into a bowl.

6 Pour a generous amount of vegetable oil into a heavy pan, and heat over medium heat to 150°C/300°F, or when a small piece of bread browns in about 20 seconds. Add the cookies and deep-fry until golden brown. Drain the cookies on kitchen paper, then dip into the cinnamon syrup. Arrange on a serving plate and dust with the ground pine nuts before serving.

Cook's tip
• Although getting the cookies to form the right shape can seem difficult at first, it will become much easier with practice. Don't lose heart!

Per portion Energy 669kcal/2827kJ; Protein 9.7g; Carbohydrate 126.5g, of which sugars 60.7g; Fat 17.3g, of which saturates 1.8g; Cholesterol 0mg; Calcium 154mg; Fibre 3.2g; Sodium 498mg.

Yakwa are among the best known and most traditional sweets in Korea. Light and crisp, these cookies have a unique taste created by a combination of maple syrup and sake, complemented by a delicious hint of ginger. Delicious served with a cup of green tea. **Serves 4**

Sake & ginger cookies

250g/12oz/3 cups plain (all-purpose) flour
45ml/3 tbsp sesame oil
25g/1oz fresh root ginger, peeled and grated
90ml/6 tbsp sake or rice wine
90ml/6 tbsp golden (light corn) syrup or maple syrup
2.5ml/½ tsp white pepper
30ml/2 tbsp pine nuts, finely ground

vegetable oil, for deep-frying
salt

For the syrup
250ml/8fl oz/1 cup water
200g/7oz/1 cup sugar
30ml/2 tbsp honey
5ml/1 tsp cinnamon

1 Sift the flour and add the sesame oil. Mix in the grated ginger, sake, syrup, pepper and a splash of water. Knead into an elastic dough. Roll out on a floured surface to about 1cm/½in thick. Use a biscuit (cookie) cutter to cut out the dough.

2 Place the water, sugar and honey in a pan, and add a pinch of salt. Bring to the boil without stirring, then add the cinnamon and stir until the syrup thickens and becomes sticky. Pour into a bowl and set aside.

3 Grind the pine nuts to a fine powder in a mortar and pestle.

4 Place a generous amount of vegetable oil in a pan, and heat over medium heat until a small piece of bread browns in about 20 seconds. Add the cookies and deep-fry until golden brown.

5 Remove any excess oil and dip the cookies into the syrup. Arrange on a serving plate and dust with ground pine nuts.

Per portion Energy 719kcal/3027kJ; Protein 6.7g; Carbohydrate 119.8g, of which sugars 76.9g; Fat 25.1g, of which saturates 3g; Cholesterol 0mg; Calcium 111mg; Fibre 1.9g; Sodium 67mg.

Index

Acknowledgements & epilogue

Publisher's acknowledgements The publishers would like to thank the following for permission to reproduce their images: p6 Chad Ehlers/Alamy; p7t Panoramic Images/Robert Harding; p8 G.P. Bowater/Alamy; p9t André Seale/Alamy; p9b Photosynthesis/Alamy; p10 WizData inc./Alamy; p11 Photosynthesis/Alamy; p12 Network Photographers/Alamy; p13b Mediacolor/Alamy; p14t Chad Ehlers/Alamy; p14b Life in Asia; p15 Life in Asia; p16l Robert Harding Picture Library/Alamy; p16r John-Léo Dugast/Still Pictures; p17 John-Léo Dugast/Still Pictures. All other photographs © Anness Publishing Ltd.

Author's acknowledgement The author would like to express his sincere thanks to Thomas Nelson for all his assistance and countless valuable contributions to this book.

Epilogue Korean food, whether the spicy national dish of *kimchi* or a mild temple meal of rice, is characteristic of Korean tradition. Everywhere there are contrasts, but also an overwhelming sense of balance. Ancient philosophies have helped to shape a vibrant modern cuisine, one filled with a surprising and delightful fusion of ingredients and cultural influences. From the snacks sold by street vendors, to the most elaborate royal table settings, Korean food reflects the fiery disposition of its people and rich diversity of its environment. The great Indian poet Rabindranath Tagore (1861–1941) wrote a poem praising the glorious past of Korea and prophesizing its bright future:

O Korea
You were the shining light of Asia
In the Golden Era of the Orient
And that lamp is waiting
To be lighted once more
For the illumination of the East